Reagan

The Political Chameleon

REAGAN
The Political Chameleon

EDMUND G. (PAT) BROWN

and

BILL BROWN

PRAEGER PUBLISHERS

New York

Published in the United States of America in 1976
by Praeger Publishers, Inc.
111 Fourth Avenue, New York, N.Y. 10003

Library of Congress Cataloging in Publication Data

Brown, Edmund Gerald, 1905-
   Reagan, the political chameleon.

   Includes index.
   1. Reagan, Ronald. 2. California--Politics and
government--1951-   I. Brown, Bill, 1922 or 3-
II. Title.
F866.2.R39B72   979.4'05'0924 [B]   76-271
ISBN 0-275-23040-6

Printed in the United States of America

Contents

Introduction   *1*

1. From Hollywood to Sacramento   *9*

2. The Mini-Memo and
   Other Oversimplifications   *22*

3. The Professional Amateur   *35*

4. Reagan on Taxes:
   Robbing the Poor to Feed the Rich   *51*

5. Politics in the Classroom   *68*

6. Quick-Draw Justice   *88*

7. The Dark Side of Mr. Good Guy   *107*

8. The War on Welfare   *124*

9. No Time for the Disadvantaged   *136*

10. The Inner Circle   *150*

11. Does Reagan Add Up?   *168*

Index   *177*

Introduction

Six years ago I wrote, "I am chilled to the bone at the possibility of Ronald Reagan someday becoming President." The prospect, frightening though it was, seemed remote. I never dreamed that Richard Nixon would be driven from the White House in disgrace and that an appointed President would be in office when the Presidential year 1976 rolled around. Had there been no Watergate Nixon presumably would have finished his second term in firm control of a huge political slush fund and with enormous power within the Republican Party and total control of his own campaign forces. There is no reason to doubt that Nixon would have been able to choose his successor and all but choke off effective challenge. Nixon never displayed any fondness for Reagan and no knowledgeable observer could conclude Reagan would have been Nixon's choice.

It was obvious that Reagan was positioning himself to take advantage of any opportunity that might present itself. He was getting ready to run, but he was faced with running against a favorite son of the monolithic Nixon forces, not a particularly bright prospect. Then came Watergate and

1

Nixon's personal disaster. It was a brand new ballgame, a much better one from Reagan's point of view. While he played coy for nearly a year, it became increasingly apparent that Reagan was, in fact, going to run.

After ten months in rehearsal, the Ronald Reagan show opened last November 20 at the Washington Press Club. The sun-tanned and carefully groomed former movie star surprised no one with the announcement that he was a candidate for the Presidency.

His audacity in pitting himself against an incumbent Republican President for the GOP nomination made few waves. That act had already been explained away by campaign aides. Gerald Ford had no national mandate, they said, only an appointment to the vacant vice-presidency and then automatic succession when the man who had appointed him resigned in disgrace. The most thoroughly discredited President in the two-hundred-year history of the Republic had created President Gerald Ford. The implication was clear; such a road to the White House hardly entitled the sitting President to the courtesies due an incumbent.

The campaign theme sounded again and again: Americans are fed up with their government and their leaders and are eagerly awaiting a modern Messiah. Ronald Reagan clearly regards himself as that new leader.

Most Presidential hopefuls announce in their home state, but Reagan, with his sure theatrical instincts, chose Washington, the home of "the enemy" as he sees it, in which to launch his campaign. He then followed up with somewhat anticlimactic announcements in Florida and New Hampshire, two states where early primaries may hold the key to Reagan's chance for victory.

The announcement was a brilliant theatrical performance carefully and professionally designed to suit the deadlines of the mass media and most especially the three national network evening news programs. As I watched that evening I realized that my fear now was in a fair way of becoming a reality. It suddenly seemed necessary to update my earlier book on Reagan.

I must confess that this is not an objective book. In the same breath I insist that it is not prompted in even the smallest way by any residual rancor over Reagan's defeat of me for the Governorship of California in 1966. It is, stated as simply as possible, a look at Reagan's political record and philosophy from a specialized point of view—one former Governor of California assessing the record of another.

Reagan's candidacy makes it necessary that the man's record be examined. Voters may then compare it with the shining promises enshrined in "The Speech," Reagan's carefully burnished call for all "Good Guys" to join his crusade. This is doubly urgent because of the undeniable charisma of the man and his extraordinary ability to use the mass media to project his own good guy image.

He is the self-appointed leader of "Us," and the enemy is always "Them." They can always be vanquished by diligent application of copybook maxims, the simplest kind of solutions to the most complex problems. The Speech makes good conservative listening. It tends to satisfy yearnings for instant solutions that are common among troubled Americans today. It is the same speech that was perhaps the only highlight of the Goldwater campaign in 1964. The Speech precipitated Reagan into his role as a citizen politican ready to do battle with the evils of government and set the country straight in the process.

Make no mistake about it, Reagan believes The Speech. He should; it has served him well since the mid-1950s, when he did a 180-degree turn from his liberal political philosophy and became a spokesman for General Electric. It cast him as an ardent partisan fighting for untrammeled free enterprise as the solution to all our problems. This unswerving belief is, in my judgment, a fair measure of the man's intellectual capacity. It is my hope that it is no reflection on his intellectual honesty.

Reagan's simplistic approach is dangerous enough when

applied to his favorite domestic targets; contemplation of its impact when applied to foreign affairs sends those chills up my spine anew. Reagan has already said he would tell the Soviets, "Hey, fellas, out" of Angola, leaving to the imagination of his listeners what he would do if the Soviets failed to get out. Reagan sees every situation in stark black and white terms, and he has demonstrated time and again his impatience with those who disagree. Foreign affairs involve the rights and dignity of sovereign states. We may disagree with the aims of others, and that is proper. Fortunately for the world, most disagreements are negotiated, and not by saying, "Hey, fellas, out" to the opposition. There is no room for the quick-draw artist in the diplomatic arena; the stakes are always too high and the penalties too dear.

James Reston has said that Reagan's "theater politics won't do now," and I fervently hope Reston is right. He posits that The Speech alone won't get it, that Reagan will now have to enunciate not only the things he opposes but the things he favors. It will not be enough, Reston feels, to be the beguiling voice of opposition to the appointed Republican President and all Democrats. Reston reasons that Reagan will be forced into taking specific positions on myriad questions that he has thus far ignored. I would be comforted if I agreed, but it didn't work out that way in California, and I see no reason why it will nationally.

It is difficult to think of Ronald Reagan as anything but an actor, because that has been his profession for so many years. Politics and the hard realities of political and governmental life, with all the awesome responsibilities they entail, are brushed aside by Reagan as he plays his role. His administration as California's Governor for eight years demonstrated clearly that Reagan sees his position at center stage, a standard-setter who is above bothering with details. These, he reasons, can be left to the supporting cast and extras, while he exerts super-salesmanship to convince the public that sloganeering is synonymous with accomplishment, hence what has been said has also been accomplished.

It is true that the hard-nosed national press corps will put him over the jumps, but it is far from certain that they will succeed in forcing Reagan to declare himself in anything approaching a positive fashion. It is also open to considerable doubt whether a hard-line approach will be viewed by the electorate as legitimate inquiry or prejudiced hectoring of a hero by the suspect "liberal" press corps.

The current widespread disquiet about politicians and the press tends to work in Reagan's favor. Despite eight years in Sacramento he manages to convey the image of the citizen-statesman dedicated to straightening out the mess, a gallant crusader riding into battle. There is a temptation to observe that he really never has become involved sufficiently in the processes of government to become an authentic political figure. If politicians are suspect, so is the press, at least in some quarters. It is easy to think of Reagan's destroying his enemies in the "phony liberal eastern establishment press" with a series of snappy one-liners aimed at audiences that want fervently to believe in this quixotic new leader. It happened in California; it could happen nationally.

Reagan's approach to actual problem-solving has always been simplistic and superficial. Through the years he has hammered away at the basics of The Speech, creating the erroneous impression that the problems have, in fact, been solved by application of Reagan's good guy philosophy. There seems little reason for him to change this tactic.

Reagan continues to trumpet his accomplishments, and many people appear to believe him. They have little opportunity to discover the truth. I note in my travels that people outside California tend to think Reagan's record is just as advertised. This was confirmed by the Harris Poll on January 8, 1976. Only 21 per cent of those polled believed Reagan would be against the working man, the poor, and minorities; only 20 per cent see him as an arch-conservative, and only 26 per cent see him as too close to big business. Reagan has been able to escape the taint of extremism and arch-conservatism that smothered Barry Goldwater. These startling figures can only mean that Reagan's superb skill as a communicator has created a false image of the man and that his record is being ignored.

Reagan's pre-announcement campaign was carefully tailored to show him before only the friendliest of audiences: organized Republican women and certifiably conservative business and industrial groups. His speeches were always received with warm and uncritical approval and sometimes with wild applause. It is impossible to calculate what effect this show of approval might have had on voters through mass media exposure. The tactic is, of course, a sound one and reminiscent of Barry Goldwater's repeated tours of Orange County during the 1964 Presidential campaign. Goldwater haunted Orange County not because he needed to mine additional support in that citadel of conservatism, but because film reports on national television conveyed the impression of wide and growing support.

The tactic was unavailing in Goldwater's case, but Reagan is another kettle of fish entirely. He is so utterly in command of himself on television, due mainly to those long years before the cameras, that he creates an aura of plausibility that always eluded Goldwater. Given the fact that Americans are legitimately concerned about inflation, the cost of government, crime, foreign entanglements with all their unpredictable consequences, proliferating social programs and their costs, and a wide range of other vexing problems, Reagan may have found a fertile field in which to plant his ideas.

It is a cruel hoax to encourage the belief that our gravest problems can be solved simply and without substantial reordering of everyone's priorities at costs that may be heavy. The prosperity of the majority of Americans has given birth to a revolution of rising entitlement among those less fortunate. The disadvantaged continue to press for real opportunity, and they rely heavily on advanced social welfare programs to provide them with both sustenance and a chance to develop new skills. It would require unacceptably radical surgery to change this. To do so might well present the nation with a set of new and more insoluble problems.

There is widespread opinion today that the liberal programs of the past forty years have failed. Undoubtedly, better solutions should be sought, but that does not mean a complete reversal or abandonment of the historic concern Americans have shown for the poor and oppressed. Oddly, many people, including Reagan, who got their own second chance as a result of liberal federal programs to help the poor and the unemployed are today leading the attack against these very programs. The "every man for himself" doctrine they preach is dangerous, heartless, and downright un-American.

My first book on Ronald Reagan was written at the end of his first term as Governor of California. It dealt largely with his record as Governor and its effect on the state. This book will deal with Reagan's promises versus the reality of his accomplishments and, most important, with the exaggerated and unwarranted claims he continues to make about those accomplishments. Reagan has cast himself in a much larger role this time, and this analysis will weigh Reagan in relation to national and international affairs. His record in California makes a useful microcosm for study, especially since Reagan's early days of campaigning find him preaching the same old line in an expanded form.

I have no ongoing political ambitions. I retain a deep and abiding faith in the American system of government. I speak as a man who has had a lifelong commitment to public service, a continuing commitment, although I am now in a different role. I served the State of California for eight years as its Attorney General and eight more as Governor. This experience equips me, I believe, to render critical appraisal of the Reagan years and put them into a proper national perspective.

In that process I have tried carefully to avoid advancing my own philosophy as an alternative to Reagan's. The limited references to events during my administration in California are cited solely to illuminate the realities of the Reagan years. They are not intended either as appeals for vindication of my views or irrefutable evidence that Reagan is wrong. Comparisons have been unavoidable in some instances, however. They are made solely to illustrate the vast gap between Reagan's frequently callous attitudes and what I still believe to be the mainstream of American thought about the duties and obligations of society toward its unfortunate members, who, from time to time, need the help of their government.

I reaffirm my belief in the nobility and worth of democratic government and the enduring merit of the American political system. Even with all the warts and imperfections that have become apparent our system stands tall. It is my belief that it is threatened most seriously by the unreasoned attacks of simplistic self-servers who pander to the lowest urges that plague our troubled people. That is why I have written this book.

1
From Hollywood to Sacramento

The first responsible suggestion that Ronald Reagan would make a good candidate for high public office came on the heels of the Goldwater debacle in 1964. The late Frank Jordan, then Secretary of State of California, sent up what was widely regarded as a trial balloon suggesting that Reagan would make a good gubernatorial candidate for the GOP in 1966.

The press was incredulous and amused. Granted, Reagan, who had campaigned widely for the Republican candidate, had emerged from the Goldwater disaster not only unscathed but with his own reputation greatly enhanced. Granted, Californians had elected actor George Murphy to the United States Senate two years earlier; but surely this was an aberration that would not be repeated. How could anyone take Reagan seriously as a major political candidate?

At the time he stumped for Goldwater, Reagan was best known as an actor of no notable consequence whose political philosophy appeared as stable as a weathervane on a windy day. Once an outspoken liberal, his espousal of conservatism began when he took to the promotional road for General Electric, sponsor of his TV series. It is easy to imagine the corporate giant making plain to Reagan that his speeches to its dealers' meetings were to be foursquare for free enterprise and cold to any advanced social doctrine. For Reagan the actor, the GE spokesman spot probably began as simply another role to play; if they wanted motherhood, apple pie, and fair trade laws, that was what he would give them.

Reagan was a great hit with the GE dealers. The address he delivered in these appearances (The Speech, as it became known to its detractors), was equal parts Horatio Alger, Alice in Wonderland, and Frank Merriwell. It struck a responsive chord with many people, most of them arch-conservatives. From these appearances it was an easy move into politics as a smooth spokesman for the right wing. Reagan found new acceptance and perhaps even a new respectability in the role. It was, after all, an extension of his regular movie role, the good guy pitted against the forces of evil. He quickly became the most articulate and sought-after advocate of conservative dogma, and he offered the same simple solutions that had delighted GE dealers. They continued to delight his new audience.

Reagan's name began to appear more and more frequently in news stories as a potential political candidate, but he still was referred to as "actor Ronald Reagan" in most if not all cases. It was apparent that most qualified political experts did not take his prospects seriously. Since I was one of those who refused at that time to regard Reagan as a real threat, I feel entitled to point out how wrong we were. I have the political scars to prove it. It should also be noted that these experts were, in the main, the same group who prematurely wrote Richard Nixon's political epitaph after I defeated him for Governor of California in 1962 and he delivered himself of the famous "you won't have Richard Nixon to kick around any more."

In retrospect it seems that the press and many other experts misassessed public reaction to actors stepping offstage and into serious roles. It was generally considered that continual references to Reagan as an actor—and especially when they went on to make clear that he was no Oscar winner, no boxoffice draw and no international star—would have a demeaning and disparaging effect. The actual effect may have been the exact opposite. Reagan had always played the guy in the white hat. Hindsight now suggests that voters carried that image throughout the campaign and into the voting booth. This was just one of many areas where the conventional wisdom failed.

In the 1966 Republican primary, Reagan coasted to an easy victory to become the party's gubernatorial nominee. Nonetheless, I greatly underestimated Reagan as the campaign approached, as did some of my advisers.

We had our neat, logical reasons for thinking that Reagan would be easy to beat:

- He was a fading, aging actor who had never really gone very far beyond roles in grade-B movies and whose most recent prominence was as the host for the mediocre "Death Valley Days" TV series.
- He had never run for nor been appointed to any public office and was completely inexperienced in the field of government.
- In his adult life, he had flip-flopped from enthusiastic advocacy of ultraliberal Democratic causes and candidates to a firm and fond embracing of far-right-wing Republican celebrities and attitudes.
- His only recent political exposure had been his unqualified and widely televised support for the 1964 Republican Presidential candidate, Barry Goldwater, who was trounced in California as well as nationally.

Ronald Reagan for Governor of California? Absurd!

But win he did, and Ronald Reagan's 1966 victory over me for the Governorship of California was neither a political fluke nor simply the result of a periodic swing of the

political pendulum. The majority of Californians were ripe
for a radically different type of Governor and immensely
receptive to the personality, style, and philosophy of
Reagan.

Let us look closely at the significant elements of that
campaign, particularly those Reagan is counting on today in
his run for the Republican nomination for the Presidency of
the United States.

One of Reagan's early advantages was that he was not
identified by the public as a politician. The brilliant GOP
state chairman in 1966, Gaylord Parkinson, had successfully
established what he called the "Eleventh Commandment" in
the Republican Party and campaigns: "Thou shalt not
speak ill of any Republican." There were deep divisions
within the Republican Party philosophically, and sharp
personal antagonisms between some of its leading figures,
but Reagan, Parkinson, and others managed to create an
impression of harmony and unity. Their method was
simple. Unlike the Democrats in California and elsewhere,
who seem habitually and openly to be at each others' throats,
the Republicans screamed at each other and hammered out
their differences behind closed doors, then came out to face
the cameras for arm-in-arm "unity" press conferences.

Reagan has made it clear that he intends to apply the
doctrine of the Eleventh Commandment in his run for the
nomination against Ford. (His presence in the race, of
course, is a strong suggestion that he finds the candidacy of
the incumbent less than exhilarating.) Reagan himself can
afford to stand above any gut-fighting, because the
Republican right will be mobilized on his behalf perhaps as
never before, even in the days of the Goldwater campaign,
and it is not difficult to foresee situations where the gloves
will come off. Reagan's support may in fact be as narrow as is
argued, but it is granite-hard, amply financed, and includes
the largest number of working volunteers within the GOP
ranks. Many are the same people who worked in the trenches
for Goldwater a dozen years ago. They are battle-smart and

tough. Few if any of them have any respect for the Eleventh Commandment, and the campaign promises to be a tough and dirty one. Theirs is a must-win situation; there is no compulsion to be polite, let alone fair, if that might jeapordize victory.

This is a most unfortunate time in our nation's history for the kind of divisive campaign that almost certainly will result. Americans are still traumatized by Watergate and related events, shocked by disclosures of illegal activities by the FBI and CIA, dismayed by unflattering facts coming to light about past presidents and other high officials, and frightened by the sagging economy and high unemployment. A mud-slinging campaign will do nothing to restore faith in America's leadership or political system. Most especially, in the post-Watergate climate of suspicion and doubt, a leader who attempts to stand above and apart from the actions of his followers will be performing a striking disservice.

Traditionally, Americans tend to be suspicious of politicians and government. That element of mistrust may remain submerged when things are going well, when the economy is booming and political leaders convey an impression of personal force or magnetism. But if the people are uneasy or angry about the tide of social events, if the taxes are hitting them hard or the economy is faltering, or if their leaders seem indecisive or, worse yet, boring, the antipolitics instinct surges to the surface, and the "rascals" are likely to be thrown out.

By 1966 the temper of the people of California had been undergoing a gradual but profound change for three or four years. The voters were confused and upset by events that seemed beyond their comprehension and beyond the control of their leaders. John F. Kennedy was assassinated in 1963. In 1964 the University of California at Berkeley exploded in student turmoil and protest, and the public's indignation rose at the portion of its taxes going to pay for the education of "those damned kids." Watts burst into flames, bloody violence, and racial fury in 1965, and ghetto riots also occurred in the Hunter's Point district of San Francisco; fear became rampant among white citizens who tended to equate black unrest with all crime, which was rising sharply, and to turn all the more against rising welfare and antipoverty costs.

At the time of his first campaign, Reagan sensed that there was a new surge of disdain for politicians in the land and uninhibitedly proclaimed his contempt for politicians and politics. "Let's take politics out of government," he said again and again. Such a move would be about as easy as taking the flour out of bread, but in 1966 the majority of Californians were receptive to Reagan's antipolitics stance.

The deep social and racial tensions that were emerging in California in 1966 were cleverly exploited as Reagan and other Republicans painted the Democratic state administration as "soft" on black violence, student riots, and general lawlessness. There was intensified public resistance to government spending in California in 1966, and Reagan pinned the blame for increasing governmental costs on Democratic "irresponsibility" and not on the actual growth of the state. California was also one of the first major political battlegrounds of the "law and order" issue. Reagan proclaimed, "We must preserve and enforce law and order."

Californians were turned off by ghetto violence and student turmoil. Confused, fearful, or threatened, they did not want any qualifications added to the simple call for tough law enforcement. They wanted a candidate to set his jaw firmly, pound his fist on the rostrum, and demand, without qualification or elaboration, "law and order." Reagan offered that firm stance and promise in the campaign of 1966.

The dozen years that have passed have traumatized Americans as few other periods in their history have done. The malaise of 1966 seems to have reached almost epidemic proportions today. The economy has been in a tailspin for several years; the rates of both inflation and unemployment continue high. Problems of race and poverty remain unsolved. The crime rate continues to rise. The Vietnam War has ground to a welcome but inconclusive end, and the complexities of a foreign policy of détente are more difficult for the average person to grasp than the rigid principles of the cold war. Despite this, there is little question in my mind that a substantial majority of Americans would turn their backs on a transparent demagogue like George Wallace were he to offer simplistic solutions to our problems. I am nowhere near as certain they will also repudiate Reagan, given his image and extraordinary personal salesmanship.

Another major underlying change in society partially accounted for Reagan's victory in California in 1966, and, I believe, Nixon's victories nationally in 1968 and 1972. In essence, the Democratic Party has contributed to its own defeats in recent years by helping to create an affluent society. For more than thirty years, the Democratic Party aligned itself with and sought to advance the cause of the underdogs in the nation—the poor, the suppressed minorities, the struggling workers, and the intellectuals who allied themselves with the disadvantaged. After three decades of policies, programs, and budgets, the Democratic Party had helped to broaden affluence in the nation and reduce, numerically, the biggest source of its political strength. Today there are fewer poor, the blacks and other minorities have made substantial advances socially, and the "struggling" worker has two cars in the garage and a boat in the driveway. The underdogs of the nation, even counting their intellectual allies, no longer constitute anywhere near a political majority. Democrats retain a substantial edge over Republicans in formal voter registration, but the registration figures are becoming meaningless when citizens move into the booth to vote. The nation is still blemished by pockets of poverty and groups kept out of the mainstream of American life, but the increased militance of the poor, the blacks, and their student allies has antagonized the majority of affluent, tax-paying voters. Politically, the American underdog is today passé. In terms of the surface attitudes and opinions of the people, the Democratic Party today may be the minority.

Ronald Reagan masterfully articulates the complaints, fears, antagonisms, and suspicions of that new majority. He not only has become its spokesman but also has given an open respectability to views that the majority wasn't quite sure were acceptable in the context of American values. Ronald Reagan rode into power in Sacramento as a latter day Matt Dillon, ready to rid the state of the modern bandits and troublemakers. He still rides the same horse. But today we face problems on the national scale that surpass in seriousness and difficulty of solution those of any one state, problems as unsusceptible to Reagan's simple formulas as were those of California, as we shall see.

Social scientists tell us that the average American is preoccupied, understandably, with such personal concerns as his family and his job and gives only superficial attention to politics and public affairs. This is why Reagan's personal abilities as a communicator give him an enormous advantage over any other political figure, whether me in 1966 or President Ford in 1976. Reagan is the absolute master of two-dimensional politics, a product made to be sold on the home screens of television.

The prototypical American politician, conditioned by years of direct contact with the people, finds it difficult to adjust to television. He is a proud man who winces when experts spread makeup over his face and tell him what to say. He operates partly by instinct, hunch, and empathy and does not like the invasion of technology into his imprecise realm. He is exuberant in the midst of crowds of human beings but is depressed by the metallic and pasteboard clutter of television studios. He needs to see the faces, or at least sense the mood, of the audience; now he must gaze at the glass eye of the camera and respond to the clinical curiosity of the media men. Instead of speaking from his heart, he must now read from the electrically controlled teleprompter placed just above the camera. With a pragmatic attitude and proper coaching, the prototypical politician can cope with the new milieu of television, but he resents the middlemen and machines separating him from the people.

Ronald Reagan relishes the new two-dimensional television politics. He is not a new breed of politician but rather a natural exemplar of a new and radically different type of politics. Its prime characteristic is the dominance of the simple surface appearance of men and human affairs, rather than the deeply complex realities of humanity.

Reagan is fitted for this new political realm by reason of both his professional experience as an actor and his personal characteristics. For almost thirty years he polished his acting talents in the movie and television studios of Hollywood, never attaining the first rank of his profession but achieving a comfortable competence in front of the cameras. (When first informed that Reagan might run for Governor, his former boss, Jack Warner, replied, "No. Jimmy Stewart for Governor. Ronnie for best friend.") For two-dimensional politics, Reagan is also blessed with surface qualities that are immediately appealing: a resonant voice with a tone of natural sincerity and just the right touch of boyishness, a hairline as unmoving as the Maginot Line (Gerald Ford once quipped, "Reagan has prematurely orange hair."), and a ruggedly handsome face that is neither unusual enough to jar the viewer nor so deeply wrinkled that it can't be smoothed out with makeup. He will be sixty-five years old in 1976, but most people would probably guess, from his appearance, that he is ten to fifteen years younger than that.

Many politicians who were accustomed to the more traditional, personal methods of campaigns are today deeply concerned about what they call "packaged politics," the process by which the candidate is placed completely in the hands of image-making experts and, with little chance to assert his own identity, presented to the voters as an attractive package. Reagan, I am sure, does not share the concern. He is the package. He arrived on the California political scene already possessing the neat, colorful, and attractive wrappings that would delight any public relations professional.

Reagan's talent for the simple quip fits neatly into the needs of television news. With occasional excellent exceptions, television normally feeds the audience a sequence of brief items that barely scratch the surface of facts and understanding. The savvy political leader knows that, when he makes a major, lengthy statement on some important public issue, he'll be lucky if it gets twenty seconds of attention on the evening news. He is asked by television newsmen to sum up his views on some vital social issue in thirty seconds. It helps if the politician is negative, if he condemns or attacks, rather than outlining positive and constructive ideas and proposals. His comments will then be considered more entertaining by the news editor, and he might rate a full minute on television instead of a few seconds.

Reagan feeds the voracious appetite of television for the simple, easily understood, negative capsules of news that media executives assume the audience wants. His two-dimensional characteristics keep him prominently on the television screen and help sustain his popularity. One myth about Reagan that is eagerly accepted by his critics is that he is publicly effective only in a controlled, rehearsed situation, as in a motion-picture or television studio, when the script is already prepared and the direction is expert. In fact, Reagan is extremely poised and effective also in the free-flowing give-and-take of a press conference or any other unrehearsed question-and-answer session. His mind, though confined to simple and rigid dogma, is quick, and there is little hemming and hawing before he offers an answer. He is capable of temperamental outbursts, but rarely loses control while on camera. He seems to follow the old Nixon dictum that a politician should never show anger except for dramatic effect. Reagan seems, and undoubtedly is, relaxed in most unrehearsed television programs or news conferences, sustains a tone of almost light banter, and often comes through with a change-of-pace joke to enliven the proceedings for his audience. Despite his informality, he conveys a sense of strong conviction and sincerity, which is perhaps his greatest asset in the unrehearsed television program. He appears to be calm, confident, and unharried, but also earnest, concerned, and dedicated. I would sum up his style in front of the camera as "cool intensity"—perhaps the perfect quality for a politician in the McLuhan era of communication.

Reagan leaves little doubt that he is constantly aware of the big audience. Most politicians tend to relate—logically and emotionally—to the individual reporter who is asking questions, or a bit more broadly with the newspaper he represents. Reagan relates primarily and continuously with the television audience. As a trained actor, he is able to ignore the clutter of equipment and commotion of reporters at a press conference and keep his eye and a good part of his mind on the audience represented by the small lens of the camera.

The two-dimensional politics of television is transforming attitudes toward public issues as well as public personalities. With the new emphasis on the appearance—the superficial physical features—of individuals, Americans are being conditioned now to judge the worth of a cause less on its intrinsic merits than on the fashion of its advocates' clothes or their hair styles. I am afraid that the new two-dimensional politics is conditioning Americans to make up their minds on the basis of their first quick, superficial reactions to style and taste rather than of rational consideration of facts and ideas.

The unsettling question is whether or not there is anything inside the Reagan package. Is the most important reality and identity of the man the attractive wrapping itself, the surface appearance? Appropriately, I think, Reagan titled his autobiography of a few years ago *Where's the Rest*

of Me? If he doesn't know, how can anyone else, including
the voters, be expected to know what's behind the attractive
wrapping of the Reagan package?

There are two great ironies in the Reagan campaigns and
his subsequent performance as Governor of California.

The first is that, for all his belligerent negativism, his
antigovernment attitudes, and his emphasis on the wrongs
of the world, Reagan came across to the majority of
Californians as a positive man. Unlike Goldwater, Reagan
never suffered from a reputation for shoot-from-the-hip
negativism. Philosophically and politically, Reagan pours
his energies into attempts to denounce, restrain, or cut back.
But personally, Reagan conveys an impression of
positiveness. To many Californians, his voice is sincere, and
his actions seem cloaked in genuine conviction. Recent polls
confirm that this impression prevails nationally.

I too would allow that Ronald Reagan is undoubtedly a
sincere man. I also believe that he is in reality what he
appears to be: a simple man. His ideas, his philosophy, his
perceptions, his comprehension of human affairs and
society are also neatly confined to a simple framework of
thought and action that permits no doubts and
acknowledges no sobering complexities. No wonder his
manner is that of a man with utter confidence in his own
fundamentalist purity and integrity, the efficient missionary
dedicated to eradicating evil. Unfortunately, in these times
the simple man or the simple answer is not enough.

The second irony of Reagan is that, for all his expressed
contempt for politics and politicians, he is an instinctively
talented and increasingly skilled politician. In 1966 he
correctly read, sensed, understood, and knew the public
mood and what the people of California wanted. There can
be no all-inclusive definition of politics, but mastery of
politics must include the achievements of getting elected,
influencing a majority of the people, and sustaining personal popularity. Reagan has achieved all three.

There are others less charitable than I who believe Reagan

just acted out the part of Governor of California during the working day but never became really involved beyond the point of learning his lines. These people hold that Reagan is an ever changing product of his own environment, a chameleon whose coloration changes with his surroundings. They point to his political flip-flop from left liberal to ultra-conservative and note that the changes coincided remarkably with his changing environment and peer group substitution. The beginning of Reagan's rock-ribbed conservatism can be traced to his days as a GE spokesman—of that there is little question. Earlier, he had shed his liberalism when Red-hunting government committees struck terror among actors and others in the film business. I am persuaded by these arguments, but I still cling, perhaps naïvely, to my belief that Reagan is a simple, honest man despite his flip-flopping. I can testify that he was a successful political candidate, whatever the case.

But it is one thing to be a successful candidate and popular personality, and another to be an effective leader. In the moments of truth when a leader sits in the corner office of the Capitol and must, by a stroke of the pen or nod of the head, decide complex issues and difficult questions, the lives and the futures of people hang in the balance. That is not a simple responsibility. In the final reality of leadership and public authority, a leader needs more than a smile and a quip to govern wisely and well.

2
The Mini-Memo and
Other Oversimplifications

Ronald Reagan's personality and professional style are inextricably intertwined. They were molded during years of work as a Hollywood actor who experienced short periods of intense work and long layoffs between films. Reagan made money at his craft, plenty of it, and obviously enjoyed his frequent long vacations. During many of his years in the motion picture industry he lived on a ranch in the Malibu Hills above the San Fernando Valley, where he carried his cowboy roles over into real life. This was a life he loved: horses, cattle, open space, an uncomplicated and uncluttered existence of the sort coveted by a great many people but affordable by only a handful. He made no bones about enjoying his way of life, once telling an interviewer:

"Lots of actors sit around after the day's shooting, have a few drinks, and gab. As for me, when we wrapped for the day I headed for home."

It is my belief that Reagan saw his years as Governor as an extension of his acting career, that he perhaps subconsciously perceived it as his biggest starring role, playing the Governor in a life-size, statewide production, but only during the working day. Certainly every public figure becomes, in effect, a role-player who must learn to ad lib effectively in the many situations where no script is available. However, most become immersed in the job, and the role-playing becomes less and less a conscious act. As they broaden their grasp on the intensely dramatic situation in which they must function, they devote more and more of their time and energy to the task. Personal lives almost disappear, a fact to which any political figure's wife, including my own dear Bernice, will willingly and vocally testify. This never happened in Reagan's case. After hours and on weekends he was the same old Ronnie Reagan, actor, with a 9 A.M. call to the "set" in Sacramento.

Reagan had always been a performer. He was a capable actor usually cursed with bad films, not a bad actor as some critics assert. His efforts on behalf of General Electric and Twenty-Mule Team Borax were essentially acting chores. Whether he was advocating the senatorial candidacy of Helen Gahagan Douglas against Richard Nixon, as he did with ardor in 1950, or Barry Goldwater's Presidential effort in 1964, he was always center-stage, the consummate performer and a communicator of great skill and poise. Small wonder this carried over into his own campaigns and into his years as Governor.

Reagan did his utmost to preserve his Hollywood style of life during his years as Governor of California. He was known as a basic nine-to-five executive who delegated a very considerable amount of responsibility and authority to subordinates. He tried to keep his evenings free and, whenever possible, retreated to his Los Angeles home on weekends. It was an open secret among his staff and the press that he never really enjoyed the rubber-chicken-circuit events that are so much a part of public life and that he assumed only unwillingly the responsibility of attending a minimum number of functions that absolutely demanded the presence of the Governor.

Reagan's reluctance to immerse himself utterly in the

responsibilities of being Governor was coupled with his adherence to a set of simplistic right-wing maxims anchored in limited concepts of patriotism and fundamentalist human values. Being a simple man, he could accept the idea, long ago abandoned by more sophisticated public servants, that there were simple answers to the questions a Governor must answer. This attitude, which pervaded his staff as well, was epitomized in a startling device originated by the Reagan Administration: the mini-memo.

The mini-memo worked this way: When a political, legislative, social, or economic issue required a decision by the Governor, his staff prepared a one-page summary of all its aspects, concluding with a suggested decision. It was divided neatly into four succinct paragraphs, one each for "The Issue," "The Facts," "The Discussion," and "The Recommendation." There was enough space at the bottom of the page for Reagan to pen a check mark to indicate either "yes" or "no" on the recommendation.

He and his staff boasted about the mini-memo as the ultimate efficiency, a method by which the Governor became informed and through which he decided. They maintained that there was no issue facing the Governor of California that could not be boiled down to a one-page summary for decision-making. They have, when pressed by incredulous reporters, stated that sometimes Reagan did spend longer periods for "discussion" of an issue. One might hope so!

Brevity is often appropriate in the attempt to condense, digest, and understand masses of information, and it is possible that some variation of the mini-memo could be one, but only one, useful informational technique for a Governor. What is frightening about the Reagan mini-memo is the near-exclusive reliance his administration placed on it and the extent to which it represented the broader attitude of Reagan that there are quick and simple answers to the complex questions of government and society.

Any good political leader must place reliance on his staff

for information. There are limits, however, and these are transcended in the mini-memo concept. This places far too much faith in condensed staff views and leaves little room for examination of the facts that formed the opinion. It has come to light that Richard Nixon placed the same sort of blind reliance on certain top aides with results that are well known. No chief executive can shut himself away from the broad range of pros and cons and accept a capsule version of problems and solutions without losing track of reality. Such attempts to create sanitized intellectual environments, uncluttered by basic information, are no less dangerous with Ronald Reagan at the center than they were with Richard Nixon.

I shudder at the thought. The decisions of a Governor are not just expressions of his personal philosophy or exercises in some game of politics. Those decisions affect—sometimes profoundly or critically—the lives of human beings. How could any conscientious man easily decide, after glancing at a one-page summary, whether or not to grant clemency to an individual who is scheduled to die in San Quentin's gas chamber? How could one page sum up the merits and weaknesses in a proposal to spend millions of dollars for some new and untested program to feed the hungry, or train the unemployed, or care for the sick? How could the questions involving the deep conflicts between races and the explosive challenges of the young be understood from the reading of a mini-memo?

The Governor of any state faces problems every day that cannot be reduced to a single volume, let alone a single page with one neat paragraph offered as the solution. Only unmitigated arrogance, ignorance, or a total lack of concern could account for the development and implementation of such a system. It is carrying the "simple solution" notion to absurdity.

Consider, if you will, the consternation that would grip cabinet members—the Secretary of State, Defense, Agriculture, or Treasury—if they were required by a

President to reduce all problems to a single page and then suggest a solution in "twenty-five words or less" as dictated by the mini-memo. It is likely that most problems confronting a President cannot be premised adequately in a single page, let alone laid out, backgrounded, discussed, and solved. If they could be, someone else would already have solved them.

Of course, it is possible for a zealot or an ardent partisan of almost any view to encapsulate his position, because such an individual does not feel any constraints to be objective or to suggest alternatives. I submit that this is not the kind of information that prepares an executive, public or private, state or national, for adequate decision-making. Despite these flaws, Reagan and his aides prize the mini-memo system.

A paradox emerges in a careful study of Reagan's performance as Governor and public figure. Publicly and personally, he gives an impression of simple, comfortable, and confident decisiveness; seldom does any doubt arise that Reagan knows right from wrong and that he is taking the right side. But substantively, on many urgent and important issues, he is often ambivalent, inconsistent, evasive, and indecisive, while on other issues, usually those that have already aroused public wrath, Reagan, not at all vague, jumps in with simplistic and rigidly moralistic judgments about the most sensitive and volatile problems facing the states and the nation. That's what is perhaps most distressing, for anyone who is concerned about the health of representative, democratic government, about Reagan's significance as a successful politician today. The scary thing about the man is the immense gap, if not the clear contradiction, between the public's impression of what he is and the reality of what he has said and done in public office.

Sacramento newsmen often left his press conferences feeling that the Governor had spoken clearly and decisively and then, examining their notes, discovered that his words were noncommittal. On March 5, 1968, Reagan offered a long statement praising the old Civilian Conservation Corps and leaving a distinct impression that he favored a similar program at the state level to put unemployed young men to work on conservation projects. But when reporters studied the transcript, this is what they found:

REAGAN: . . . It is a job that could be done if you had the facilities and the means to do it. Now, in our own summer jobs, we are thinking in terms of fire trails and the stepping up of a program of hiking trails in our wilderness areas and so forth. . . .

QUESTIONER: This sort of thing requires money, though, Governor. Have you allocated anything in your budget to it?

REAGAN: As I said, we are looking at that one. . . .

Some of Reagan's remarks made Spiro T. Agnew seem like an inarticulate Milquetoast by comparison. Commenting on the tragic and complicated pattern of Negro ghetto riots, Reagan said, "These are no longer riots connected with civil rights in any way. These are riots of the lawbreakers and the mad dogs against the people." Answering a question about campus disorders, he said that student militants are "part and parcel of revolution," and then added: "If it takes a bloodbath, let's get it over with. No more appeasement." When asked about labor union leaders who had complained about the use of state prisoners to harvest crops, he answered this way: "Sometimes they remind me of, you know, a dog sitting on a sharp rock howling with pain [that] is too stupid to get up." Angered by the late columnist Drew Pearson's charges of a scandal involving Reagan's staff, the Governor said that Pearson "had better not spit on the sidewalk if he returns to California."

Repeatedly during his years as Governor, Reagan displayed a skill with the grisly *bon mot*, a far cry from his stylish and funny one-liners turned out by script writers and committed to memory. In 1974, for example, when poor people were squabbling over food giveaways during the efforts to ransom Patricia Hearst, Reagan said: "It's just too bad we can't have an epidemic of botulism." There are substantial numbers of people who regard this as a fair sample of Reagan's true attitude toward the poor, and indeed toward any group he comes to regard as troublesome.

To some extent, I sympathize with any Governor or public official whose occasional bloopers are joyfully played up in the press. Reagan is still trying to live down one comment he made several years ago during a controversy over the size of a proposed national park for northern California's redwood groves. He was quoted as saying, "A tree's a tree. How many do you have to see?" There are moments, in the furious pace of an election campaign or in the flurry of questioning at a press conference, when the words don't come out quite as the speaker intends.

A slip of the tongue is excusable, but a cynically or carelessly simplistic statement on a sensitive public issue is unpardonable. One of the most sensitive and volatile issues to face society in recent years was the pattern of student unrest, demonstrations, and occasional violence. The pattern began in California and for at least three years was acute on the state's campuses. Where the crisis of campus unrest cried out for calm, firm, but fair comment and leadership, Reagan chose instead to play the role of an indignant propagandist. In the case of the People's Park controversy in Berkeley, for example, his angry rhetoric, I believe, contributed as much to campus turmoil as the excesses of radical campus agitators.

Reagan's official authority in the controversy was limited. He did act properly when, at the request of local leaders, he imposed a curfew in Berkeley and called out the National Guard to help restore order. But, at the most volatile moments of the crisis, he also fanned passions with references to the need for "bayonets" to quell the turmoil, with condemnation of harried university administrators as "appeasers," and with blanket indictments of all those who

supported the People's Park project—idealistic en-
vironmentalists as well as radical agitators—as "the mob."

I am no less critical than Reagan of the violence-
advocating militants on campuses or anywhere else. But a
political leader in today's free American society is not just a
Commander-in-Chief whose only duty is to shout "Charge!"
when segments of the society challenge authority. That, in
essence, is all Reagan did in the People's Park tragedy. In any
volatile social upheaval, a leader's public stance and
statements will tend either to inflame or to calm passions. In
today's restless society, one of the key responsibilities of the
public leader is to serve as a conciliator of conflicting
groups. Reagan is more intent on picking one side and
fighting with it. His erroneous statements on the People's
Park tragedy were a battle cry that misled the people. Here
are just a few samples:

REAGAN: At no time did the squatters [on the university-
owned lot] even designate an individual or a
committee with whom the Chancellor could communicate.

FACT: Student Body President Charles Palmer repeatedly
contacted the Chancellor to discuss the crisis, and, on
May 14, the People's Park advocates did form a
committee to negotiate with the university.

REAGAN: Now it has been learned that part of the lush
greenery that was planted to make the lot a so-called
sylvan glade turned out to be marijuana.

FACT: Neither the police nor any other authority produced
evidence that marijuana plants were growing in
People's Park.

REAGAN: There are no shortages of parks in Berkeley.

FACT: At the time of the People's Park turmoil, there was
no park at all serving the area.

Reagan is equally simplistic and intemperate on much
larger issues. Several times in the past few years, he has

publicly, explicitly, and firmly equated the possible use of
U.S. nuclear weapons with the firing of muskets at Concord
Bridge at the onset of the American Revolution. "There
comes a time," he said in a discussion about the potential use
of nuclear weapons, "when we have to take a stand against
the Communists." All of our recent Presidents and most
citizens who have spent any time at all thinking about the
destructive power of nuclear weapons regard their potential
use with extreme caution. Not Reagan. When questioned
about some actual or implicit threat from Communist
nations, Reagan usually invokes an obscure, parenthetical,
out-of-context quote from Dwight D. Eisenhower to the
effect that we ought to make the enemy believe and fear that
we are ready and eager to use nuclear weapons.

It does not require much imagination to know how
Reagan would react to some international threat or crisis. He
has already confessed knowing little about the Angola
problem but favors "eyeball-to-eyeball" confrontation. After
the U.S. intelligence vessel *Pueblo* was captured by the
North Koreans, America debated the facts and issues
involved. Ultimately, and after patient, tedious, and delicate
negotiations, the captured crew members of the *Pueblo* were
safely returned home, and an open armed conflict with
North Korea was avoided.

How would a President Reagan have handled the delicate
Pueblo crisis? The answer is revealed in his press conference
of January 30, 1968:

QUESTIONER: Governor, a few days ago you were quoted as
     saying that you would have given North Korea
     twenty-four hours to release the *Pueblo* and prove
     that we were going to go in and get it. I wonder if you
     would clarify for us whether under the circumstances
     you would anticipate armed resistance . . . and if so
     whether this would endanger the lives of the eighty-
     three [crew members].
REAGAN: Well, first of all, no one wants to endanger the

lives of the eighty-three. . . . I think that what we are ignoring in this climate of recent years is the moral obligation, the sacred obligation of government to protect any individual, wherever he may be in the world, if his rights are being unjustly imposed upon by someone else. That's the purpose of government, to provide the strength of the collective citizenry to go to the aid of any one of us. And now it is the aid of eighty-three of us—and I said twenty-four hours. . . . There is no moral justification for this country standing by and letting what amounts to an act of piracy, an act of war, be perpetrated upon us and write off eighty-three young men. . . .

QUESTIONER: My question was, Governor, that if you've made the ultimatum we are going in to get them, what would you anticipate happening? Would the eighty-three still be alive for us to rescue? Would you want to bomb the port where the ship sits? Take the city by force?

REAGAN: You are asking for specifics that I've just told you I don't think anyone can give who doesn't have access to the advice of the Chiefs of Staff about such an incident. But if you are going to be overly concerned... as to whether the enemy is going to retaliate in any way—when they are in truth the criminal, they are guilty—then I'd like to ask what number do we set the limit on? How many of our citizens can be kidnapped by a foreign power before the rest of us decide that they have reached a point in which we have an obligation to do something about it? . . . I do know what the limit is in my mind. I think the limit is one. . . .

QUESTIONER: Can I phrase it just one more time? Then do you think it is possible to get back our eighty-three men forcibly without a very dire jeopardy of their lives?

REAGAN: Yes, yes, I do . . .

This is the essence of the Reagan style, a fast draw, a lightning shot, and off for home and hearth. It would be unfair, perhaps, to quote Reagan on national issues of a few years ago, except that it was always Reagan who precipitated the situation by offering his opinions, solicited or otherwise. This is a vastly different Reagan from the poised and polished platform presence, carefully groomed and wrapped in a slightly conservative but stylish tailored suit, snapping off the one-liners. The Reagan who likens "one tree" to all trees and suggests that botulism would be welcome under certain circumstances is the man behind that benign mask.

There remains an important unanswered question as to whether the Reagan style and personality can accommodate to the rigors of a national campaign. His understandable zeal for a private life may be ill-suited to the rough and tumble of the national campaign trail. Primary campaigns in many states are not media-dominated. It is still necessary to get out and press the flesh, look the voter in the eye, and go to breakfasts, lunches, dinners, *kaffeeklatsches*, and a plethora of other time-consuming events. Following at your heels, always, is the unrelenting press, eager for new information and probing for weakness, ambivalence, ignorance, or switches in the line. Rain, snow, hail, overheated halls, hostile audiences, hecklers, and the overbearing presence of the federal security people, with the implicit suggestion that danger is never far away—these are the facts of national campaigns, along with a full bag of uncountable annoyances, and they take their toll.

I recall Henry Cabot Lodge's defense in the unsuccessful Nixon campaign of 1960. Lodge simply snuggled down and took a nap every afternoon, changing into pajamas and ignoring any demands on him. This amused the press, enraged Nixon, and befuddled the professionals, unused to candidates who could not be bullied or cajoled into working twenty-hour days.

In the past Reagan has managed to convey the impression that he was dragooned into serving as a candidate. It is consistent with his style to accept a draft rather than press hard for nomination. His abortive and amateurish bid in 1968 was a source of embarrassment to him, and it remains to be seen how well he can play the role of a candidate who must bid for the nomination.

It is safe to assume that he would have preferred going to the Republican Convention in Kansas City to accept a nomination thrust upon him by a deadlocked convention, but that possibility was foreclosed by Gerald Ford's early and seemingly unequivocal declaration. As this is written, Reagan's success in the primaries is a matter of conjecture. It is clear, however, that he will be marked up in the fight, not by Democratic opposition, as in his California campaigns, but by a sitting President with ambitions of his own, a partisan following, and the staggering power of the White House impelling him onward.

Conventional thinking holds that Reagan's over-simplifications will not wash with the informed electorate, that his hard-core support may not be much larger than that around George Wallace. There is evidence to support this theory, at least in part, but much of it uses the Goldwater debacle as its base and point of departure. Adherents of this theory hold that Reagan's candidacy is simply Goldwater revisited but that this time around the battered but enlightened majority in the GOP will turn aside this new challenge by the right.

I am not especially comforted by this theory. I think it fails to give appropriate weight to Reagan's capability as a salesman-communicator. It also underestimates the unease afoot in America today. And I think it totally ignores a first maxim of political reality, which holds that a candidate must be electable to be worth anything.

Reagan's simplistic oratory is a soothing syrup for the minds of disquieted, worried, and confused voters. It is quite natural for people to believe what they want to believe, and Reagan appeals to our desire for comfort and deliverance from fear. Since the campaigns are barely under way as I

write this, I must qualify these remarks by saying that I am
not a seer, so I cannot predict what might happen to alter the
balance as I see it now. I regard Ford as an uninspired
political leader, thrust into his present prominence by the
worst political tragedy in American history. The latest polls
bear out my fears that Reagan is a most formidable
opponent. He will remain so, barring the unforseeable
cataclysm.

Before we pass to the examination of Reagan's record as it
really is written, I must make one additional observation,
and there is no need to qualify this view in the slightest:
Ronald Reagan's election to the Presidency would be a
national disaster.

3

The Professional
Amateur

Ronald Reagan was elected Governor of California as an
amateur, and he professes to be one today, more than nine
years later. It is difficult to understand how, let alone why, he
clings to his amateur standing after eight years in the
Governor's office, an aborted Presidential bid in 1968, and a
year of "noncampaigning" for the 1976 Republican
Presidential nomination, which took him to thirty-four
states. But he does.

In continuing to call himself an amateur or "citizen"
politician, Reagan applies the same logic the Soviets do
when they declare their Olympic athletes to be amateurs
despite overwhelming evidence to the contrary. Reagan
remains an amateur simply because that is what he wishes to
be or, more important, what he wishes to be considered by
the voters. This wishful clinging to amateur standing is
indicative of Reagan's distrust and fear of professionals in
government and in politics. In June 1973 Reagan voiced his
displeasure this way in a speech to university students in
California: "I was a little disappointed that, in about three
weeks after I was elected, I had automatically in some

people's minds become a politician. I still don't think about myself as such."

Reagan has frequently expressed contempt for politicians and has resisted the notion that he became one the day he filed in 1966. He has always expressed admiration for professionals in business and bigness in industry, yet he equates professionalism and bigness with badness in government. A clue to the genesis of this fixation can be found in this Reagan quote from an interview in 1973:

> One thing our Founding Fathers could not forsee— they were farmers, professional men, businessmen giving of their time and effort to an idea that became a country—was a nation governed by professional politicians who had a vested interest in getting re-elected. They probably envisioned a fellow serving a couple of hitches and then looking eagerly forward to getting back to the farm.

There is doubtless plenty of room for argument over what the Founding Fathers envisioned, but more curious than this pre-emption of their attitudes by Reagan is his own compulsion to continue in public office rather than "return to the farm." It is difficult to square his ambitious plans for himself with this expression of his professed attitude. Even though he now aspires to lead the government, he continues to express fear and distrust of it and at the same time frequently reveals a warped concept of what government really is. The Founding Fathers, realists about human nature, wrote various checking mechanisms into the Constitution so that the men elected to govern would have enough power to do the people's will but would not be able to exceed their proper authority. In that speech to the students in 1973, Reagan said, "Our Constitution is a document that protects the people from government." The Constitution surely loses in Reagan's translation.

Reagan's obsession with the virtues of amateurism

extends to the bureaucracy as well as politicians. He appears not to know that government agencies by the dozen are run quietly and efficiently by longtime civil servants whose expertise is essential to the operation. Speaking to students in March 1973 Reagan expressed his attitudes this way:

> One of the things that is wrong with government is this idea that there is a certain group of people who will make a professional career out of government. That's fine, but we also must always have an influx into government of people-citizens who say, "I owe the community something and therefore I will give one year, two years, three years—a period out of my life to serve my community and bring to government the thinking of the man on the street, the people out here who sometimes say "why is government doing this?"

While the quote rivals some of the utterances of the late Casey Stengel for lack of clarity, it would appear that Reagan is suggesting a bureaucracy composed of amateurs along with amateur leadership. All of these amateurs would be just plain people, if Reagan had his way, armed with no special expertise but simply a will to serve. That implies Reagan has great faith in the people, but that is not necessarily the case. Here's a Reagan quote from another speech to students in June 1973: "The people who hold public office today are no better, no worse than the people who send them to public office, and you cannot expect them to be. They are representative of you."

Reagan appears somewhat confused, if one can judge from these quotes, but his antiprofessional theme remains intact. In October 1972 he said it clearly: "Government is too important to be left to those who are not too busy—the professionals who think government has some sort of divine right to tell people what is good for them." Despite his scorn for professionals he has always adopted professional techniques in the furtherance of his own political ambitions. He has been on the campaign trail since leaving the

Governor's office a year ago, yet he coyly insisted for more than ten months that he had made no decision about running against Gerald Ford. As one wag put it: "Reagan is just doing what every ex-Governor does: criss-crossing the country, making political speeches, and meeting with every political group he can. Naturally he is surprised when anyone suggests he may be a Presidential candidate just because he is going through all the motions of a candidate."

Many avowed professionals do precisely the same thing, and I have no quarrel with Reagan over the tactic. My complaint is against his lack of candor and his insistence that he is not a professional despite eight years as Governor of the biggest state in the Union. I also suspect that his reluctance to disclose his candidacy until virtually the last minute might have had something to do with his radio show, which netted him a handsome six-figure income. Once he declared, the show was subject to the equal time rules of the Federal Communications Commission, and that meant it had to be pulled off the air.

This conduct is consistent with the Reagan style, as was his denunciation of "big government" in his announcement speech, an almost anticlimactic declaration of a candidacy that had become a foregone conclusion. He has always attacked bigness and professionalism in government as twin evils and cast himself as a modern David against the twin Goliaths. This was his stance in 1966 and again when he stood for re-election in 1970. It should not surprise anyone that he has not changed. His claim to amateur standing may be much less credible today. Born as it was in genuine ignorance of most governmental processes and respon- sibilities, it had some appalling consequences ten years ago.

With confidence born of ignorance, Reagan equated most of the problems of society with the growth of government. In the 1966 campaign he expressed special contempt for individuals who were skilled and experienced in the craft of government. His basic attitudes were, and remain, not only antigovernment but also antiprofessional. He sneered at what he called "professional politicians" and offered the people the superficially appealing vision of leadership by the "citizen politician."

It quickly became evident that "citizen politician" in reality meant amateur Governor. As Governor, Reagan immediately showed himself to be not only ignorant of the basic workings of government but also astonishingly uninformed on the most important issues facing the state.

News reporters were remarkably kind to Reagan as he exposed his continuing ignorance of state affairs in his press conferences during the first year of his term. But the critical reader of the transcripts of those question-and-answer sessions notices an Alice-in-Wonderland quality to Reagan's remarks. The difference is that Alice, at least, had the curiosity to learn and ask questions as she wandered through a strange realm.

The examples of Reagan's exposed ignorance on important state issues are endless. At times reporters couldn't believe their ears, but Reagan was unbothered by his ignorance. Early in his administration Reagan was hopelessly confusing in one press conference on a major financial question, until the subject was ended by this exchange:

QUESTIONER: Why can't you figure out where the $40 million came from [to pay off a deficit]? You paid the money, but you don't know where it came from?

REAGAN: That's right.

In his press conference of March 7, 1967:

QUESTIONER: Governor, there's a move in the legislature now to increase the southern California share of the state highway funds from the present 55 per cent to 60 per cent or more. How do you stand on this?

REAGAN: Oh, you got one I haven't been into yet. All I know is just dimly that I know there's been this discussion and I haven't looked at it.

In his press conference of March 14, 1967:

QUESTIONER: Governor, the legislature is about to adopt a
deadline of April 11 for introduction of new bills. Do
you think you'll have the rest of your program ready
to present to them by that time?

REAGAN: Well, I haven't talked since then to my legislative
task force on this, so I don't know the state of their
preparations. I've often wondered why there are so
many laws that have to be passed and maybe we
should try to see how many we could do away with. . . .
There are only a few more things in keeping with the
promises I made during the campaign that I feel a
necessity to introduce.

QUESTIONER: What are they, Governor?

REAGAN: Oh, I'm trying to remember now. . . . I'm going to
have to check up on this and find out what still
remains.

A month later, on April 11, Reagan still was unsure even
about his own legislative plans:

QUESTIONER: Are there any of your programs, Governor,
that will not be introduced in this session?

REAGAN: You know, I honestly can't answer that. We are
trying for all of them. I would have to consult with the
task force to find out. . . . There may be some things
that have to hold over.

Also on April 11:

QUESTIONER: Governor, several other Governors have
indicated they have been offered a hot line telephone
to the White House. Have you been included in that?

REAGAN: I think we have . . . a disaster phone. There is a
disaster phone connecting Governors. I don't think

we can call in. They have to call us. When that one
rings, run for the basement. I feel like a little general
in "Beatle Bailey." Do you think I have been
overlooked?

The lack of details in his knowledge of vital issues was
revealed again and again throughout his terms in office.
Dozens of times reporters caught him with virtually no
knowledge of issues that were nearing decisions in the
legislature or commanding the prime attention of the press
and public. Running through his press conferences with
startling frequency were such remarks—on major issues—as
"I haven't thought about that yet" and "I haven't read that
report" and "You caught me on that one, I don't know."

Even when caught short on a major vital issue, Reagan
seemed reluctant to inform himself and form judgments. In
the spring of 1967 the legislature and the people were giving
major attention to a bill to reform California's law
regulating and limiting abortions. This was the sequence
of Reagan's ignorance and indifference on that issue:

May 2
QUESTIONER: Is there any possibility of a residency
   requirement in an abortion bill? Would you favor
   something like that so California wouldn't be "an
   abortion center"?
REAGAN: I never even thought about that.

May 9
QUESTIONER: Governor, the North Carolina bill has a
   residency requirement. Is this something you would
   like to see in a bill California might have?
REAGAN: I've never given that any thought. I don't
   understand. I'd not want to create a kind of attraction
   in the state for this sort of thing, but I'd never thought
   about that.

May 16

QUESTIONER: Governor, your own church denomination
    had a convention here over the weekend and they
    urged you to support abortion legislation. Has that
    changed your thinking on it in any way?

REAGAN: I'm just as confused as I was last week.

June 13

QUESTIONER: Governor, the Assembly will be voting on
    this [abortion reform] bill in less than two hours. If
    they approve it in the form it is in now would you veto
    it?

REAGAN: I've just been asked that question. I haven't had
    time to really sit down and marshal my thoughts on
    that.

Even immense public interest in the abortion reform bill
didn't seem to move Reagan out of his indifference. For at
least three months the issue drew heavy mail from citizens to
the legislature and to the Governor. That aspect was raised at
his June 13 press conference:

QUESTIONER: Governor, I understand you received a heavy
    flux of mail on this subject. Did that have any bearing
    on your thinking?

REAGAN: No, as a matter of fact, I didn't know about the
    mail. As I said, I've been out of town. I didn't know
    about the mail until I read it in the paper this
    morning.

The new Governor often revealed his determined
amateurishness by stating that there was no point in his
delving deeply into a subject because he was not a trained
expert in it. He stated that he would not attend or chair
clemency hearings (which I and most other Governors had
done) because he was not a lawyer. He was reluctant to read
several important reports or meet with delegations on
questions about the state mental health program because he

was not a physician or psychologist. Reagan seemed to regard experts in government more as convenient buck-passing devices for him to use than as competent professionals on whom he could rely. Many of his appointments indicated a profoundly antiprofessional attitude. He was asked about one such questionable appointment in his press conference of March 21, 1967:

> QUESTIONER: This week you appointed a Dinuba hardware man who was your Tulare County campaign chairman to the post of Chief of the Division of Housing and Community Development. Does this gentleman have any particular background in that field . . . in light of your statements that this administration would find the most qualified persons for the appointive offices?
>
> REAGAN: Well, if he didn't have the qualifications he wouldn't have been given the position. And it's just a remarkable coincidence that some of the most capable people also happened to support my campaign.

Reagan appears to make two exceptions to his generally antiprofessional attitude. His statements on periodic international crises, such as the *Pueblo* incident, or continuing conflicts, such as Vietnam, indicate that he favors giving immense decision-making power to expert military officers rather than "amateur" political or diplomatic officials. And, in some areas of governmental authority involving special economic interests, he often gave power to individuals he regarded as "experts" but who in fact represented vested interests. To the position of State Real Estate Commissioner he appointed a former head of the California Real Estate Association who vigorously opposed open-housing legislation. To supervise the regulation of the state's savings and loan associations and banks, he appointed an executive of a savings and loan association. He carried this pattern to the point of absurdity when he appointed to a scenic roadway board an executive of an outdoor advertising firm specializing in highway billboards.

Reagan's general solution for society's problems emphasizes spontaneous, voluntary efforts. When a private, voluntary effort succeeds, he jubilantly exaggerates its impact out of all proportion to reality. After the Watts riots of 1965 H. C. "Chad" McClellan, a southern California industrialist, organized a private effort to reduce unemployment in that Los Angeles black ghetto. He enlisted other industrialists and businessmen to offer jobs for the "hardcore" unemployed and continued the work during the first years of the Reagan Administration. Reagan was ecstatic in his praise of the McClellan effort and repeatedly held it up as proof that voluntary, private efforts could lick social problems "without a dollar of government funds." McClellan's work was indeed worthy, and he and his business allies did provide thousands of jobs for Watts citizens. But they did not "solve" the unemployment problem in Watts; the unemployment rate in that ghetto was higher in 1969 than at the time of the 1965 riots. And McClellan himself scoffed at Reagan's attitude and excessive claims, while noting realistically that both private and government programs are necessary to achieve significant progress. He acknowledged in 1968 that unemployment continued high in Watts and told *New York Post* columnist Murray Kempton that he wished Reagan would stop "playing that numbers game" in boasts about the jobs that had been found. Kempton also quoted McClellan as saying that he had found it necessary to fight against Reagan's "reluctance to understand the need for the national government." McClellan added: "Federal training programs? Hell, our trouble is we don't get enough of them. If we could double the production of the Manpower Defense Training Act skill centers, we could still get every one of them hired. Sure, I give the federal people hell frequently. But I work hand in glove with them, because I know that I have to."

Reagan assumes that businessmen can not only take on and lick most social problems but also move in on a part-time basis to achieve a pure sort of efficiency and economy in government. But there were few significant reforms or improvements stemming from the innumerable task forces of businessmen that Reagan appointed just before and after his inauguration; about all he could boast about was the saving of $100,000 through a new system for purchasing and using typewriter ribbons in state offices. Many, if not most, of the businessmen he appointed to important state positions left his administration within a year or so to return to private industry. Businessmen simply did not have the time or the interest to flock full time to Reagan's "Creative Society" banner.

One reason for the reluctance of businessmen to join Reagan's crusade with enthusiasm and sustained effort was that he had so tarnished the image of government that they too regarded it as their enemy. Well into his Governorship, Reagan continued to speak of government as if it were an alien force in society, one that should be whittled down in social significance and left with only a few housekeeping chores. I am convinced that Reagan does not just oppose the high costs of government or the cumbersome size and shape of the bureaucracy, but he considers government itself essentially evil. With such negative perceptions and attitudes, why should his followers, including many businessmen, dirty their hands in the tasks of government?

Even granting the superficially attractive quality of some of Reagan's rhetoric, there is little basis for respect of his performance in checking the growth of government. There is an immense gap between the vision of his inaugural address and the reality of what he did in the Governor's office.

On September 21, 1969, he repeated the major theme of his inaugural address when he spoke to a group of California businessmen: "Nothing is more important right now," he said, "than cutting the cost of government. This should be the top priority of every administration. I repeat, nothing is more important than economy in government." On that same day Reagan signed into law a bill giving big salary increases to state government executives, including himself.

As a Presidential candidate, he's back on the economy kick, but he shifted his emphasis to the nation some months ago. In a speech to California Republicans in October 1974, he put it this way: "Putting our economic house in order is America's greatest imperative, and it must take precedence over everything else."

The inconsistencies between Reagan's rhetoric and his performance on economy in government would be laughable except for the human consequences. In the same month that he approved the big salary increases for himself and other state executives, he chopped a $5 million appropriation for the Needy Children's School Lunch Program down to $500,000. State Senator George Moscone, the program's sponsor, noted that half a million schoolchildren in California were not then receiving the minimum food requirement for health. Angrily and appropriately, he accused Reagan of "gutless hypocrisy" for the Governor's "tactic to take the heart out of a humanitarian bill he didn't have the courage to veto outright."

There was no move by what Reagan calls the "private sector" to fill the proven food needs of 500,000 hungry schoolchildren. His expressions of fond hope that business and industry can solve the obvious problems of society are both naïve and dangerous.

Reagan, a self-styled reformer, wasted the opportunity to effect change that any Governor—whatever his philosophy—has. A new Governor enjoys tremendous political momentum. He has the respect of the legislature and the most charitable of attitudes possible among the press. For a time, perhaps as long as a year, a new Governor has the chance to transcend the usual governmental and political conflicts and to establish his own policies and programs. That period of great political potential is usually called a governmental "honeymoon" between a chief executive and the other forces that will later oppose him vigorously.

Reagan muffed the tremendous advantages he enjoyed in his first year in office. Instead of a "honeymoon," Sacramento languished in a mood resembling a slumber party. For months after the inauguration, the Capitol was in suspense and then confusion about his administration. He was extraordinarily slow in filling major state positions and in outlining vital decisions in even the routine operations of the state. Months after he took office, even Republican legislators were plaintively reminding him that a Governor had to do things, not just talk about them. I am convinced that Reagan could have pushed through a major effective tax reform program, for example, during his first year of grace before the oncome of strident opposition. Instead, he spoke only vaguely about tax reform, presented no detailed proposals, and wasted a precious opportunity for leadership on a vital issue. Seven years later, as a result of Reagan's indifferent leadership and political amateurishness, California was still waiting for a significant tax reform program.

The strongest evidence of Reagan's amateurishness—and perhaps the most damaging effect of his naïveté—is in the area of finance and fiscal policy.

In 1967 Reagan faced a specific fiscal problem—the financing of the state's new Medi-Cal program—with a stubborn refusal to employ efficient remedies. Looking back on the confusing problem and controversy over Medi-Cal, the *Long Beach Independent-Press-Telegram* reported on May 20, 1968:

> The Reagan Administration's approach to the problem of financing Medi-Cal can be likened to a man noticing that his couch is smoldering, and then running down the street shouting "Fire, fire" without even attempting to use his handy fire extinguisher.

California employs thousands of people highly
skilled in the fields of finance and administration.
Their experience could have been Ronald Reagan's fire
extinguisher. But it wasn't sought or used. . . .

If the Governor had sought advice from men
experienced and capable in state government . . . he
would not have suffered the public embarrassment of
having first a Sacramento Superior Court and then the
State Supreme Court tell him he was acting illegally [in
cutting out Medi-Cal services].

The ink used to write the final figures for Medi-Cal in
1967–68 will not be red, but the Governor's face should
be.

Reagan is capable of believing anything he says, and this
led to one of his biggest financial blunders. In the year
following his election he inherited a deficit, although it was
much smaller—about 154 million dollars—than the billion
dollars he estimated. He failed to take into consideration the
fact that the state was on the accrual system of accounting
and would pick up a large portion of the deficit as monies
flowed in from taxpayers of all classes. Reagan at first
attacked accrual accounting, then admitted on March 7,
1967, that "there's nothing wrong with the accrual
bookkeeping system." He persisted, however, in going
ahead with a massive tax increase totaling $1 billion and
found himself with a $537 million surplus, the largest in the
state's history.

Later he discovered the truth of what I had told him: that it
is impossible to enact a tax reform measure in an election
year, when half the state senate and all of the assembly are up
for re-election. While he raised taxes repeatedly after that, he
did not do so in election years. Had he listened to that bit of
professional knowledge I offered, he would have understood
that the deficit he inherited was far from critical and was, in
truth, close to liquidation without his embarrassingly large
and unnecessary tax increase. I also pointed out that State of
California bonds were rated AA during my administration,

reflecting the confidence of the financial world and belying Reagan's bankruptcy charge. Again, he ignored me.

During the early days of Reagan's Governorship Franklyn Nofziger, now his Western campaign director but then his press secretary, conceded that Reagan and his closest aides were not only amateurs but "amateur amateurs." They learned a few things, granted, but the amateurism persisted, as witness the debacle when Californians rejected Reagan's prized Proposition One, a gimmick by which voters could have set limits on their taxes. Reagan hoped to use Proposition One as the heavy gun in his Presidential campaign, but the voters saw through the superficial and dangerous scheme and turned it down. Reagan was largely to blame himself, since he campaigned vigorously for the proposition but admitted time and again that he didn't really understand it. This was a kind of amateurism the public didn't like, and it cost Reagan heavily in prestige and public favor. The same amateurism led him to spring his $90 billion tax transfer plan without adequate research and with apparently little personal thought to its implications, and once again Reagan paid the price in credibility and prestige.

Despite his continued claim to amateur status Reagan did learn a good deal about politics, as anyone who watched his shy posturing throughout most of 1975 would admit. He perceived his niche accurately and from the start set out to position himself to the right of Gerald Ford, no mean feat, given the tiny space available along that part of the political spectrum. He saw his support as mainly among the far right, the disappointed but still hopeful Goldwaterites who refused to accept the lesson of 1964 and who live in hope of bringing back the nineteenth century. He was right, of course, and the first Gallup Poll since his official announcement reflected that bedrock, hard support and put him ahead of President Ford.

I would observe that Bo Callaway's angry denunciation of Reagan at Houston in December 1975 showed clearly who the amateur politician was on that day. Reagan had another one-liner when asked if the poll that showed him leading might have touched off Callaway's attack. "I don't know why he should be upset," Reagan smirked. "I saw that poll, too, and it didn't upset me."

I would submit that Reagan is no amateur either at government or politics, but he is still an enemy of government, fearful and distrustful and dedicated to tearing down the orderly processes without having adequate substitute machinery ready to put in their place.

Call this amateurism if you wish. It is my judgment that it is cynical political opportunism, which we can ill afford. I once likened Reagan, the "citizen politician" with his ardent love of amateurism, to a "citizen pilot" at the controls of an airliner. Both would be crash-prone, I said then.

The comparison remains apt.

4

Reagan on Taxes: Robbing the Poor to Feed the Rich

In his zeal to identify "big government" as his main target, Ronald Reagan came out swinging with a scheme to cut back the federal budget by $90 billion even before he officially announced his 1976 Presidential candidacy. That was in September 1975, and Reagan was nothing more than a highly visible and vocal "private citizen" at the time. His plan attracted scant attention then, but as these words are written it looms as his first revealing and potentially serious error in his run against President Ford.

The theme is reminiscent of Reagan's familiar pledge to "cut, squeeze, and trim" California's budget and taxes, made during the campaign of 1966 and repeated *ad nauseam* through the next eight years. The facts are that taxes rose steadily, as did state budgets, each year of Reagan's two terms in Sacramento. Unfortunately, the public perception of Reagan as a budget-slasher and tax-cutter lingers on, precisely because he keeps talking about instituting enormous economies but never alludes to his record of failure to fulfill his promises.

It appears that Reagan agrees with that arch-cynic H. L.

Mencken, who referred to American voters as boobs ready to follow a leader down any primrose path provided his promises were glowing enough. It is a view I never have shared, but Reagan appears to have adopted Mencken's theory that it is impossible to go broke "by underestimating the intelligence of American voters."

Reagan's shotgun blast at the federal budget, delivered before the partisan and receptive Executive Club of Chicago, called for "a systematic transfer of authority to the states" in many areas now considered federal domain, including welfare, education, Medicaid, and housing, among others. The plan showed precisely where the federal budget could be reduced as a result of such transfers. Since it is doubtful that even as many as a corporal's guard among the most conservative Americans favor total abandonment of these programs, it must be assumed that the programs would have to be continued and funded by state and local governments. How the states could pick them up after a federal withdrawal and where the money to finance them would come from are questions Reagan failed to answer.

The program was conceived by Jeff Bell, a thirty-two-year-old Reagan aide who specializes in developing issues and who appears to have developed one in this instance that is vastly different from what he had in mind. The national press began to come down hard on Reagan and his plan shortly after he announced his candidacy, and there is reason to believe it will continue to probe for answers.

Bell himself has said he expects the press to be "very rough on major proposals like this." His purpose, he says, was to "distinguish Reagan from other people and set a theme for the campaign." He certainly succeeded in that modest goal, but someone, perhaps an older and wiser head in the Reagan organization, should have pointed out that Reagan was not utterly indistinguishable from Gerald Ford in any case. The Ford campaign organization could scarcely believe its good fortune. Press Secretary Peter Kaye, an old Reagan-watcher from the staff of the Copley Press flagship, the *San Diego*

Union, admitted that the staff was "making a detailed analysis of the proposal, and the results will be made available to reporters and Ford campaign chairmen." It is easy to assume that the analysis will cast Reagan as a know-nothing hell-bent on destroying needed federal programs out of an unreasoning hatred of the bureaucracy, only to set up fifty mini-monster bureaucracies in the states. It would be equally easy to forecast far greater administrative costs resulting from this sort of foolhardy dismantling of federal government programs and an even bigger tax burden to be borne by the very same taxpayers.

Now this Reagan proposal is, on its face, cynical and ill-conceived as a means of attracting attention to a noncandidate who was, at the moment, trailing badly in the polls. Once made, however, such proposals are hard to back away from. They return regularly to haunt a candidate. There is absolutely no possibility under the sun that the Congress would permit such a program to be undertaken, and there is very serious doubt that it would meet with the approval of a single state administration. The danger lies in a different direction, that being the impression voters might form after only a superficial examination of the scheme. As I have pointed out, Reagan has considerable personal ability as a communicator, and skill in manipulating the two-dimensional politics of television gives an advantage to a superficial candidate. He is already claiming he was misquoted and his plan was "distorted."

Because of his strong salesmanship abilities, Reagan's spoken words are frequently taken as accomplishments. Let me give you one example. A friend called me recently and remarked in the course of the conversation that Reagan apparently has made a strong impression as a budget-cutter on working people around the country. He told me he heard this from people in several different cities on a recent trip, even from a cab driver in Washington, D.C., who had said: "That Ree-gun cut the hell out of taxes out there in California. I'm for him if he can do that here."

My friend, who knows better, was astonished, and asked the cabbie if he hadn't heard that taxes had gone up every year that "Ree-gun" was in office.

"I heard that, but I figured that was just those pinkos on TV knocking the guy."

I still say Mencken was wrong in his assessment of the intellectual powers of American voters, but I confess that a few out there come close to bearing him out.

The simple truth is that Reagan promised to cut taxes but failed for a variety of reasons. He certainly is not blameless in his failure, but it would be less than fair if I did not point out that factors beyond his, or anyone's, control were and always are at work against the professed tax-cutter. My quarrel is not with Reagan's failure; rather, it addresses itself to his irresponsible promises and endless repetition of them, whether in legislation or the ill-conceived Proposition One, in a callous attempt to lull the public into thinking that he could deliver on those empty promises.

At first his failures were the results of bungling and ineptitude as he overreached himself in a role for which he was ill-prepared. Californians watched in dismay when, shortly after taking office, Reagan naïvely suggested that state employees might work without pay on established state holidays. The laughter had barely subsided (the suggestion was, of course, totally ignored) when he announced a mandatory 10 per cent slash in all state budgets that same year. Months later, after doing dubious battle with the legislature, which was trying desperately to educate him to the realities of the situation, Reagan had to sign a state budget 10 per cent higher than mine had been a year earlier.

And so it went, year after year; promises of new and startling economies followed by tax increases and budget increases, even though several vital and badly needed state programs to aid the unfortunate were slashed beyond conscience (a subject we will deal with later). Perhaps the best evidence of this upward budget spiral is the accompanying table, prepared by the state department of finance.

You will note from the table that total expenditures for state operations increased by $1.3 billion over the eight years (this figure actually took a slight dip in 1970), while the percentage of those expenditures in relation to the total budget declined. At the same time you will see a rise in local assistance (monies returned to local governments by the state) both in dollars and percentage of the total budget. Note that total expenditures increased by substantially more than one hundred per cent in the period.

CALIFORNIA BUDGET—THE REAGAN YEARS
(in billions)

Fiscal Year	State Operations	% of Total	Local Assistance	% of Total	Total Budget
1966–67	$2.2	48.0	$2.4	52.0	$4.6
1967–68	2.3	45.6	2.7	54.4	5.0
1968–69	2.5	43.9	3.2	56.1	5.7
1969–70	2.7	42.8	3.6	57.2	6.3
1970–71	2.6	39.2	4.0	60.8	6.6
1971–72	2.6	39.3	4.1	60.7	6.7
1972–73	2.9	39.4	4.5	60.6	7.4
1973–74	3.4	35.6	6.2	64.4	9.6
1974–75	3.5	34.5	6.7	65.5	10.2

So the fact is that during the Reagan years the State of California's total budget increased every year, rising by 5.4 billion dollars from 1966 to the fiscal year 1974–75.

Figures of that size boggle my mind and, I am sure, the minds of most Americans. Few people have any real concept of how much a billion dollars is, let alone an astronomical 5.4 billion. Let me put it this way: This nation is two hundred years old this year. That increase in the California state budget under Reagan amounts to more than $52 per *minute* since the founding of the Republic!

Reagan and others will argue, and with justification, that California was growing, inflation was running at a brisk rate, and the bureaucracy was stubbornly resistant to efforts to curb growth or roll back payrolls. I do not quarrel with those contentions; in fact, I can empathize if not sympathize, and I can add the fact that a staggering number of federal and state-mandated programs grandfathered by law into the budget preclude any meaningful cutting. Once again, I quarrel only with Reagan's cynical attempts to perpetuate his image as a cost-cutter.

It is also interesting to note that, while state costs were declining as a percentage of the total budget (although rising when expressed in raw dollars), local costs were always on the rise. This is because Reagan fulfilled one campaign promise—that to reduce property taxes—but at the same time had to raise many other taxes at the state level to fund the programs stripped bare by the slash in property tax revenues. It was a classic "shell game," a kind of financial sleight-of-hand which passed out tax relief in one motion and snatched the money back with the next. County and city budgets continued to rise, as did tax rates at both levels.

One other word on this subject: Property tax relief benefits a single class of taxpayer, the property owner. The bigger the property owner, the bigger the relief. The hard core of Reagan supporters was and is to a very large extent wealthy people, and wealthy people own a great deal of property. It should be pointed out also that these people have a considerable edge in the effort to avoid other taxes, such as income and sales levies. While Reagan's so-called property tax reform may well have benefitted owners of single family residences, it hit them a staggering blow in other increased taxes. Big property owners realized huge savings and paid little if anything more in new taxes.

Note, too, that the Governor and his staff proposes the state budget to the legislature, not the reverse. Those ever increasing budgets during Reagan's years in Sacramento had their genesis in his office. It would be ludicrous to term Reagan a spendthrift on the basis of his budget increases, but it is necessary to illuminate the situation as it actually existed, not as he would have people believe it existed. There is something less than total honesty involved in the continuing preachment of "cut, squeeze, and trim," when the facts disclose that any such efforts to cut back government costs were unavailing. His $90 billion "plan" is the same kind of pie-in-the-sky promise.

Increased taxes, of course, are the ugly handmaidens of bigger budgets, and in this area Reagan has shown an alarming lack of candor in spreading his record before the voters. It should come as no surprise to find that taxes also increased each year of Reagan's eight-year administration. It may be eye-opening to see just how much they rose during this period of ostensible pinchpenny economy.

At the outset, let me acknowledge that inflation played a role in pushing taxes higher as the costs of government rose along with everything else. Yet the tax rise was very substantial even when adjusted for inflation. The accompanying table prepared from California State Board of Equalization figures, tells the story graphically.

CALIFORNIA TAXES—THE REAGAN YEARS

Fiscal Year	Local Taxes (in billions)	State Taxes (in billions)	Total State and Local Taxes (in billions)	Total Per Capita Tax Load (in dollars)	Adjusted for Inflation (in dollars)
1966–67	$4.3	$3.8	$ 8.1	$426.26	$426.26
1967–68	4.7	4.7	9.4	484.66	466.92
1968–69	5.2	5.2	10.4	529.56	489.88
1969–70	5.7	5.4	11.1	556.49	489.01
1970–71	6.6	5.6	12.2	605.29	508.65
1971–72	7.3	6.6	13.9	682.98	555.72
1972–73	8.0	7.2	15.2	739.82	577.98
1973–74	8.4	7.6	16.0	768.44	556.84

It is difficult to comprehend how Reagan has kept his image as a cost-cutter untarnished despite the clear record to

the contrary. Perhaps it is due in part to the natural aversion
many people have for dry statistics. They have found it much
easier to swallow Reagan's self-serving statements than to do
the necessary research that would lead them to the more
accurate conclusion that he had failed in his "cut, squeeze,
and trim" campaign. I believe that is the case in California,
and it follows that other Americans would have even fewer
facts and an even weaker impulse to check them out.

The California Constitution makes partners of the
Governor and the legislature in both the budgeting and
funding processes. The Governor is required by law to
submit his budget by January 10, together with his program
to raise any additional revenue his budget might require.
Both the State Assembly and the State Senate then go over
the budget in a painstaking and detailed study. When their
versions differ, a conference committee hammers out a
compromise. Both houses propose new revenue measures to
finance the budget, and no other measure may pass that
requires an appropriation until the budget bill has finally
been enacted. New taxes in final form are the results of
compromises. These safeguards against an unbalanced
budget force the Governor and the legislature to work
together, sometimes with considerable reluctance, but as a
practical matter they must resolve their differences in order
to get on with the business of the state. The Constitution
requires that the budget must clear the legislature in final
form by midnight, June 15.

This procedure forces both the Governor and the
legislative leadership to give very careful consideration to
the actual needs of the state. During Reagan's first term he
was handicapped substantially by not only his own
amateurism but the inexperience of people around him.
They not only misunderstood and mistrusted the complex
machinery of government, but they also remained largely
dedicated to the notion that the Governor had some almost
divine right to change whatever he wished to suit himself.
Reagan's early embarrassment when he was forced to

approve a first-year budget 10 per cent greater than he had promised should have taught him a lesson, but it did not, at least not right away. He remained basically intransigent and uncooperative right to the last.

The painful truth about governmental budgeting is that past events, continuing human needs and expectations, and the increasing demand for governmental services have a great deal more to do with the process than does either the governor or the legislature. The first six years of Reagan's administration in California were growth years for the state, although the pace had slowed from the runaway expansion that had begun after World War II and continued with only minor and brief setbacks.

After five years in office Reagan proclaimed 1972 as a year of genuine tax reform in California. What followed presentation of his budget and final approval of both that document and the whopping new tax package required to finance it became, in the words of the respected *California Journal,* "1973's fiscal fiasco."

The cornerstone of the new program, worked out in a rare spirit of cooperation between Reagan and Assembly Speaker Bob Moretti, a Democrat, was a combined tax-relief and school financing program, which the Senate accepted only after a protracted and frequently bitter battle. The plan relied heavily on a one-cent increase in the state sales tax, which went into effect on July 1, 1972, even though virtually every expert in state government said it wasn't needed at that time. But it was the foundation of the uneasy truce and for that reason was allowed to stand. The result was that the 1973 legislature returned for the first two-year session in California history to find that staggering miscalculations had been made, and the state treasury was well down the road to accumulating an unneeded and unwanted billion-dollar surplus. So much for "cut, squeeze, and trim."

Reagan's answer was to sop up the surplus, so he proposed a record new budget of nearly $10 billion, which his own cabinet admitted was "full of fat." That does not square well with his image as a penurious guardian of tax dollars, so it is never mentioned by Reagan. He tries to blame the fiasco on the Democratic legislature, but the mail from constituents indicated that this was not entirely successful at first. Speaker Moretti, for his part, said, "We gave the Governor 98 per cent of what he wanted," blaming the situation on Reagan.

At the root of the difficulty was the philosophical difference between Democrats and Republicans, especially conservative Republicans. Democrats tend to prefer income taxes, while Republicans lean toward the more regressive sales tax as a revenue-raising device. Reagan first proposed to distribute the huge surplus through a one-time personal income tax credit, but Democrats argued that this would be unfair because the surplus was generated through the increased sales tax, paid in much larger proportion by poor and low-income people. So, after much political pulling and hauling, the sales tax increase was allowed to stand and the $9.38 billion budget, larger than any other state's, was approved with plenty of cash around for a number of pet projects, some the Governor's and others the legislature's. The people paid.

Here is where Reagan's skill as a communicator, together with the much greater media access accorded a Governor than most legislators, served him well. Reagan was able to lay the blame on the legislature to a far greater extent than he should have been and thus escape, except among the more perceptive and interested California voters, any real blame himself. His thirty-second-to-one-minute summations on evening news programs around the state were far from searching examinations of the facts. They were allowed to go unchallenged for the most part by reporters, who really did not understand the situation themselves, and TV program editors whose interest lay largely in other areas. After all, they reasoned, it's just a political squabble.

I don't condemn the newsmen and the executives of the television networks and stations. Both in their roles of public service and in their functions to provide public entertainment, they must avoid at all costs (and they are involved in a business) the cardinal sin of boring the people. The people, the viewers, by and large have spent tedious and boring hours during the day on the job or cleaning the house. During the evening hours, when they turn on the news, they don't want and won't watch some repetition of the mundane.

However, this attitude on the part of the media and their audience plays into Reagan's hands. Reagan is not an educator; he is a propagandist for himself and his own narrow viewpoint. He is not a leader, but an advocate mirroring and articulating the generally right-wing attitudes of one large segment of society. I believe that, in the complexity of today's issues, a leader should seek to educate and that, in the crisis of today's polarized society, he should seek to conciliate the contending forces. Reagan not only fails in those functions, he doesn't even try to fulfill them. Reagan takes the easy path to political popularity and election success.

Reagan's presentation of himself as Mr. Cut, Squeeze, and Trim has been undeniably effective—so effective that in 1973 he deceived even himself by acting on the assumption that his *McGuffy Reader* approach to taxation and governmental economics was shared in toto by a majority of people. He was correct in assuming that virtually everyone resents paying taxes, but he was wrong in the extension of this view to the belief that they would support any sort of irrational scheme just as long as it promised to reduce their tax bills.

In 1973 Reagan took the unprecedented step of sending a tax limitation initiative to the people after the Legislature had wisely rebuffed his attempts to ram the proposal through that body. Reagan was, in his own words, taking his case to the people. The scenario was complex, but the risks originally appeared small to Reagan and his strategists. The downstream reward—the Republican Presidential nomination—would be big. It should be remembered that

this was after Watergate but before President Nixon
appeared to be in serious jeopardy. Reagan and his backers
made the then logical assumption that Nixon would finish
his second and final term, and 1976 would be a wide-open
year for Republican hopefuls. What a sure vote-getter it
would be if Reagan could tell the nation that he had given
California voters the right to impose ceilings on tax levels
and returned the control of government spending and the
power to tax to the hands of the private citizen. That was the
hope for Proposition One.

In California, as in some other states, the state Constitution may be amended by initiative; a small percentage of the
states voters through circulation of petitions may put a
measure on a ballot to be voted into law by a majority of
voters in the state. Initiative originated early in the twentieth
century, when the people needed a means of end-running
state legislatures that were "owned" by corporate interests;
too often today the initiative has become a tool with which
well-organized minorities attempt to circumvent the
thoughtful deliberations of fair-minded legislatures and to
present issues to the voters in oversimplified and often
emotional terms.

Reagan's Proposition One (so called from its position on
the ballot in a special election that cost the people of
California millions of dollars) gave California voters the
chance to approve a measure that would put a ceiling on
their future tax liabilities while gearing state spending to a
fixed percentage of the total personal income of all taxpayers
in the state. On the surface it appeared to many, including
Reagan's team, that he had a foolproof scheme to portray
himself as the white knight who had slain big government
and big spending. He flailed away at his favorite target,
profligate big government, telling voters that without
Proposition One they would be left "defenseless and at the
mercy of a vast, special-interest-oriented government
bureaucracy which voters unwittingly helped to create." He
kept harping away on the old and by then thoroughly

discredited theme that his administration had inherited a bankrupt state six years earlier, and he carefully omitted any references to his own whopping tax increase and the unwarranted surplus it created in the state treasury. He said critics of the initiative were "either not reading the measure or . . . guilty of spreading outright untruths."

All of the arguments for the measure were variations on the old theme of "too much government." One could well have believed that advocates envisioned government not as the creature of the people but as some alien body with a dynamic entirely its own and an insatiable appetite to tax. Never did they even suggest that many valued, needed, and expected state services were in jeopardy if Proposition One passed.

Assembly Speaker Robert (Bob) Moretti led the opposition to Proposition One, although I am happy to say that I also played a significant role in the fight. We were outspent by more than 5 to 1 by Reagan and his forces, so our eventual victory was even more satisfying, confirming as it did the basic faith both Bob Moretti and I had and still have in the intelligence and reasonableness of our citizens.

Moretti hammered away on his major points: First, he said with complete justification that Proposition One was an effort to reduce income taxes collected from the wealthy at the expense of the less affluent majority. Moretti made it clear that the initiative's establishment of a declining percentage limitation on income taxation would force deep program cuts and, inevitably, force future administrations and legislatures to tap other sources to continue needed services to the people of the state. He pointed out that those sources had to include sales and property taxes, both regressive and unfair to the low- and middle-income majority.

The wealthy, Moretti pointed out, already enjoyed a special advantage because of loopholes that the legislature had struggled to close but that would be reopened by Proposition One. And he made another very effective point.

Proposition One also would have written into the state Constitution a provision requiring a two-thirds majority of both houses of the legislature to raise any tax in the future. On the surface this may sound good, but Moretti again went to the heart of this matter:

> This is an attempt to impose the will of the minority and repeal the concept of majority rule in California. Under this plan, fourteen State Senators could starve out any program in this state, regardless of its worthiness and the need of the people.
>
> The legislature is closest to the people. The concept of majority rule is sound and has been for two hundred years in this nation and before that in all the enlightened nations of the world. This attempt to write minority rule into our Constitution is dangerous in the extreme and personally repugnant to me.

Well-reasoned arguments against Proposition One were put forward by respected legislative analyst A. Alan Post after he and his staff did their usual thorough analysis. They concluded that Proposition One "may well add to the total cost of government in California, with functions being carried out by the wrong level of government, using the wrong kinds of taxes and in a bureaucratic and costly manner." They pointed out in particular that existing state programs would have to be cut back by at least $1 billion in the four years following passage of Proposition One. Reagan, on the other hand, had said with questionable logic that the promised tax cut would not affect present state levels of spending, only curb increases. Post's arguments fell on fertile ground with the California State Employees Association and the California Teachers Association, which promptly joined forces to fight back. Together they raised the bulk of the $500,000 spent to defeat the proposal, and in the process forged an alliance to be reckoned with in future elections.

State employees were not the only ones who got Moretti's

message or believed Alan Post's carefully documented analysis. Senior citizens and organized labor rallied behind the opposition to Proposition One. They saw through the election strategy aimed at turning out large numbers of affluent citizens, and they heard loud and clear the message that the proposition was not, in fact, tax reform but a device to load taxes on the have-nots while the haves enjoyed even greater benefits.

Another important ally was the League of Women Voters, who took the position that a controversial and complex matter such as Proposition One should not be locked into the state Constitution, an eminently sound position. Californians have been pruning verbiage out of their Constitution in recent years, not adding to it. The league held that the initiative, untried and restrictive as it was, was dangerous language to adopt in perpetuity.

Although 85 per cent of the news media in the state endorsed Proposition One, in some cases, notably that of the prestigious *Los Angeles Times*, considerable reservation colored the endorsement. The *Times*'s endorsement was heavily qualified and carefully enumerated the basic and fatal flaws in the initiative. This sort of treatment by the responsible press did nothing to dispel the public feeling that Proposition One was the proverbial pig in a poke. Then the *Times* ran a devastating Paul Conrad cartoon which showed the Governor as "Reagan Hood," robbing the poor to give to the rich. Again, readers wondered about the real meaning of that endorsement editorial; was it an endorsement, or had it been watered down so much as to amount to opposition. The *Times* had, in recent years, retreated from the solid Republican positions it unfailingly took when Norman Chandler was publisher. His son, Otis, was a genuine middle-ground Republican, and under his leadership the *Times* had moved to the center of the road. The sort of condemnation by faint praise given Proposition One was regarded by veteran *Times*-watchers as tantamount to disapproval. In any event, the *Times* is clearly the most influential newspaper in southern California, and its less than enthusiastic approval hurt Propositon One.

With some ironic justice, the biggest boost for the opponents of Proposition One came from Reagan himself, the author of the proposition. On an election eve television program aimed at getting out the facts, he was asked, "Do you think the average voter really understands the language of this proposition?"

Reagan's reply: "No, and he shouldn't try. I don't either."

Among the audience that night were staff members of the political public relations firm Whitaker and Baxter. They seized the plum and twenty-four hours later used Reagan's self-proclaimed confusion to deliver what some observers thought was the *coup de grâce* in a series of newspaper ads.

"When a proposition's chief sponsor doesn't understand it," the ads said in part, "it's time for the rest of us to vote no."

Reagan had laid his prestige squarely on the line. His voice had been used in a tape-recorded message delivered by telephone to every registered Republican and a selected sample of other voters statewide. It was the largest use of the telephone as a campaign device ever seen in California. To confess that he didn't understand his own proposition and ask for votes on blind faith was the nadir in his show of contempt for the intelligence of the voters. The effect was devastating.

When the vote was counted the Governor's initiative had lost by more than 300,000 votes. It carried only eleven counties, ten of them among the least populous in the state. Only San Diego among the big counties voted for the initiative, and there it carried only by 2,400 votes out of a total of more than 344,000 cast.

Reagan had been wrong: You could not fool all of the people all of the time with the attractive carrot of lower taxes.

But even more important is the philosophy that guides Reagan in his efforts at what he calls tax reform. Perhaps the best way to illustrate this is to quote Bob Moretti, who talked about tax-cutting with Reagan several times during his second term in Sacramento.

"One time Reagan told me he personally favored a flat percentage to be applied universally, whether the individual's income was $100,000 or $5,000," Moretti told me. "He brushed aside my remarks that such a tax would be manifestly unfair and regressive in the extreme.

"Then he went on to tell me about Bill Holden's experience when he moved to Switzerland to avoid U.S. income taxes on all that money he took out of Hollywood," Moretti recalled. "The Governor said, 'Bill sat down with the Swiss tax people and negotiated how much he would pay. He made a deal which was good as long as he continued to reside officially in Switzerland. Now that's a great system.' I didn't bother to tell him it wouldn't be much good for poor people, because I was afraid he'd tell me in all seriousness that poor people just didn't move to Switzerland."

Intelligent and informed people know, of course, that there is growing sentiment across the political spectrum for lower taxes and government economies to match. The problem for all but the most simplistic thinkers is to find a way to curtail government services in order to make tax cuts fiscally sound. Reagan operates under no such rational restraints. He is interested only in cuts and seems indifferent to the problems that would result from curtailment of needed services. Despite the record of ever increasing budgets and taxes through eight long years as Governor of California, he has been able to convey the general impression of a great economizer. "Cut, squeeze, and trim" is only a catch phrase, with no basis in fact, yet it is associated with Reagan by a great number of people who ought to know better.

It is my considered opinion that the United States cannot afford in these parlous times to accept a sloganeer at face value, no matter how attractive that face and those slogans may be. It is my hope that Reagan will not be able to survive searching inquiry into his record.

5
Politics in the Classroom

Ronald Reagan frequently expresses boundless confidence in the abilities of the American people, the superiority of the American system, and the leadership of the United States in the world community. No superlative is too far-reaching for Reagan when he wishes to convey this confidence to an audience. Here's the way he put it in a speech to Republican Club members in January 1974: "Those nations and states which have secured man's highest aspirations for freedom, opportunity, and justice have always been those willing to trust their people, confident that their skills and talents are equal to any challenge."

These words are difficult to reconcile with the unreasoning anti-intellectualism Reagan has displayed in public office. It cannot be that he does not realize that the skills and talents of which he speaks are developed in what educators agree is the finest and farthest-reaching system of free public education the world has ever known. Six months earlier he had expressed himself this way:

I believe we have the talent and capacity to solve whatever problems we face, in the cities or in the states.

If we can land a man on the moon, develop space ships that can travel to other planets, getting people to the shopping center or between cities swiftly, safely and conveniently is certainly not an impossible dream.

Those capacities and talents of which Reagan spoke are developed to a very large extent in our splendid public education system. So are the opportunities that otherwise would be foreclosed to most young persons because they do not come from families of substantial means. Public education is costly, granted, but most reasonable people regard the cost as an investment. There is ample statistical evidence that a university education equips an individual for a better job, with greater earnings and a greater return to society in the form of higher taxes on that income. In this technological society the emphasis should be on expanding and improving both the quality and the quantity of education in the United States. Reagan's record shows him to be ill-suited for leadership in this vital area.

Ronald Reagan spent eight years in Sacramento earning his reputation as an enemy of public education and a dedicated, unreasoning anti-intellectual. He pounced on the University of California and the state college system much as Genghis Khan swept down on Samarkand, determined to leave nothing but scorched earth in his wake. Or so it seemed, as Reagan slashed budgets, manipulated the Board of Regents, and demeaned students, faculty, and administration in the most intemperate fashion.

Nobody who had listened to Reagan's attacks on higher education during the campaign of 1966 was really surprised that he proved to be less than a friend to education. However, even some of his firm supporters were astonished and shocked at the virulence of his attacks as Governor and his repeated attempts to sack the institutions by chopping them off at the pants pocket. He had, after all, said time and again he would "clean up the mess at Berkeley," but he had never said he would try to raze the university in the process.

"The mess at Berkeley" was the student unrest, which was later to spread across the country as young people, dissatisfied with many aspects of their lives, exercised the politics of confrontation, a tactic many of them had learned in the civil rights struggle in the South some years earlier. In 1964 a loose coalition of student club members representing such diverse organizations as the Young Republicans and the Progressive Labor Party, and everything in between, came together in the Free Speech Movement (FSM) to protest university action in closing a campus area to political activity. This Free Speech Movement deteriorated into a daily struggle between students and administration that from time to time threatened to shut down the campus and halt the education process. It was, in all truth, an ugly situation, and it made a superb campaign issue for Reagan. He used it vigorously, and his inflammatory rhetoric did nothing to calm the situation down. It played to the feelings of many Californians that "those damn kids ought to shut up and go back to class or get tossed out."

The university system of course makes heavy demands on California taxpayers, but there was also an emotional factor that contributed to the chasm between the generations and the public disgust for student turmoil. In California the students attending the state's university system are a minority within society, an advantaged minority. Under the law of the state plan for higher education, only the top 12.5 per cent of high school graduates are academically eligible to attend any of the various campuses of the University of California. The minority group status applies also, to a lesser extent, to the students of the state colleges, which accept applications from the top third of the high school graduates. The majority of Californians end their education with a year or two in a junior college or even stop with graduation from high school. There is, as a result, a subtle element of jealousy within the majority of the California public toward the advantaged minority who attend the state colleges and universities. Time after time, I have heard this comment from indignant citizens: "I wasn't able to go to college. Why don't those damn kids settle down and be grateful that they can go?"

I can understand and even sympathize somewhat with that point of view. I did not attend a university but went to work in my father's photography store to help the family out financially. I studied law for four years at night school, received my law degree, and passed the state bar. I am proud of those achievements, but I remain just a trifle envious of those who had the opportunity to attend a university or college.

I recall one conversation I had with a newsman friend who was covering that bitter 1966 campaign and who had also covered the first year of the FSM activities at Berkeley. I asked him if he thought Reagan really believed the vicious things he was saying or whether he was just using Berkeley and the FSM as an appeal to disquieted voters. I remember his reply very well.

"Governor," he said, "you want to remember that Reagan comes out of a solid middle-class background and attended a little college [Eureka] back in Illinois where the boys all wore letter sweaters and gray flannels, and the girls all were cheerleaders.

"He saw all those old Johnny Downs movies where Johnny, Scats Davis, Sterling Holloway, and the Preisser Sisters put on a musical show and raised the money to pay off the mortgage on old Pottawattamie. He not only saw them, he believed them.

"He is genuinely incensed when these kids refuse to button their lips and go sit in class. Beards and long hair offend him, and street politics threaten his sense of order and decency. Hell, he still puddles up when he hears the Eureka alma mater. Expecting Reagan to understand the problems of kids trying to preserve their identities at a multiversity and safeguard their guarantees of freedom is like expecting Mickey Rooney to comprehend Sagan's time-space continuum."

I didn't really buy that colorful analysis at the time, but I have come to appreciate how close it was to being accurate. Reagan went to Sacramento determined to bring his personal concept of college life to the state university and college system, and he really never stopped trying. Shortly after he was elected Reagan said, "Preservation of free speech does not justify letting beatniks and advocates of sexual orgies, drug usage, and filthy speech disrupt the academic community and interfere with our universities' purpose. I consider it my responsibility to take the lead in returning our universities to their original purpose as institutions of learning and research." That laudable, if somewhat pompous and woefully inaccurate, speech drew loud and prolonged applause. His first step down that road came a month later when the Board of Regents, with Reagan, Lieutenant Governor Robert Finch, and a Reagan-appointed regent named Allan Grant taking the lead, fired university President Clark Kerr by a vote of 14 to 8.

There was considerable press criticism of this political interference with the operation of the university system, but Reagan shrugged it off, saying, "I was only one of the fourteen votes against Kerr." There has been a continuing controversy over precisely what happened at that regents' meeting, but there is agreement on one point: Allan Grant made the motion to dismiss Kerr, and the Governor lent all of his prestige to the effort. For Reagan to call himself one among fourteen is to beg the question of the prestige of office. I wonder whether he doubted that he could have stopped the move with a wave of his hand and a dozen conciliatory words.

The shock waves spread through the academic community, and condemnation of Reagan's precipitate action was widespread. One comment will make the point, that of Kingman Brewster, Jr., the distinguished president of Yale. On hearing of the firing, Brewster said: "The political context and abruptness of the regents' action is bound to threaten the administrators and faculties of the great California system."

Reagan attacked the California university system quickly in other ways, but not without a bit of public vacillation of his own. In the first few weeks of his term, his administration initially denied Sacramento rumors that he favored a 10 per cent cut in the budgets of the university and the state colleges. Before the end of the month, Reagan's economy ax slashed even more deeply than the rumors had suggested it would. In his first budget message to the legislature, the new Governor proposed these drastic reductions:

- a cut in the state appropriation for the University of California from the $278 million requested by the Board of Regents to $196.8 million—a 29 per cent reduction
- a cut in the appropriation for state colleges from the $213 million asked by the Board of Trustees to $154 million—a 28 per cent reduction

The news media correctly reported that Reagan's program would mean a radical shift in state policy: Qualified high school graduates would no longer be assured a place in California's institutions of higher learning. And some newspapers, including the *Sacramento Bee*, correctly noted a tragic irony in the Governor's policy for higher eduction. Reagan, who had campaigned under an "Obey the Law" banner, was defying both the state law spelling out the master plan for education and the Constitution itself. He was undeterred, arguing that he was just "cutting the fat" from the university and college operations, and that the money for the requested budgets "just isn't there."

Those who looked closely at the Governor's per-formance—and remembered his recent statements about education—saw through his arguments. There was enough money "there" for Reagan to take such noneconomy steps as doubling the costs of his personal staff and office operations and of giving additional tax breaks to oil corporations operating in California. And critics knew that reductions of 28 and 29 per cent were more like chopping the heart out of higher education than "cutting the fat." The fears increased as Reagan uttered a series of statements that exposed an intrinsically anti-education attitude. Speaking directly within the context of a discussion on the higher education budget, Reagan said that he was not going to ask the taxpayers to help "subsidize intellectual curiosity." That incredible comment prompted this angry, but apt, response from a professor at UCLA: "What the hell does he think a university is all about?"

Kerr's firing and the budget cuts (partially modified after negotiations with the Regents) were not the only prongs of Reagan's attack on higher education. He proposed another drastic measure to end the established and worthy principle of free higher education in California, urging that university and college students pay tuition for the first time in a century. The tuition proposal was advanced of course, with arguments about "economy."

In more outspoken moments, Reagan revealed another motivation for the tuition proposal. While Max Rafferty was beating the demagogic drums around the state by saying that Berkeley offered "a four-year course in sex, drugs, and treason," Reagan was saying that tuition would help keep "undesirables" off the Berkeley and other university campuses. "Those there to agitate and not to study might think twice before they pay tuition," he said at one press conference.

Within one month of becoming Governor, Reagan had come up with a neat triad of reprisal-like moves, which would affect those he and the public had stereotyped as scapegoats for campus turmoil: First, Kerr's firing could not help but intimidate other "vacillating" administrators. Second, the budget slashes and other fiscal decisions would penalize all those "agitating" professors. Third, tuition charges would hit all those noisy, sign-carrying student demonstrators. The formal proposals were advanced in the name of economy and necessity, of course. But on television and in his stump speeches, Reagan cleverly and subtly boasted that he was indeed cracking down on the troublesome campuses of the state.

The shocked reaction was not confined to Reagan's political opponents or members of the academic communities. The *Los Angeles Times* became an articulate voice against his attack on higher education. In a January 1967 editorial, the *Times* put the issue into proper perspective, referring to California's "great system of higher education and the unrivaled opportunity it offers to every qualified student." The *Times* noted that California had "achieved its tremendous technological growth and resulting prosperity primarily because of its unrivaled resources of higher education and university-connected research" and warned that endangering those resources "would be the most short-sighted and destructive kind of economizing."

By March 5 the *Times* had lost all respect for Reagan on the issue of higher education. A lengthy and carefully documented editorial stated:

> He has demonstrated that he does not believe it is vital for society to enable each citizen to achieve the best in knowledge and skill of which he is capable.... An anti-intellectual political reactionary now governs California and is determined to bring higher education growth to a grinding halt.... If a university is not a place where intellectual curiosity is to be encouraged and subsidized, then it is nothing.... If the Governor is seeking to transform the University of California overnight into an institution of second rank, and if he desires to hold back the development of a strong state college system, he has chosen the right paths to reach those goals.

But Reagan was basically unmoved by the criticism (though occasionally infuriated by it), and he adamantly pursued the path of devasting budget slashes and imposition of tuition. Starting in 1967, tens of millions of dollars were cut from the budget requests for the university and college systems. The state legislature invariably approved larger and more appropriate sums; Reagan won out by use of the powerful "item veto" after legislative action. The Board of Regents at first voted against Reagan's tuition proposal, but gradually Reagan's war beat down the regents' opposition on that issue. In the fall of 1967 the board approved a slight increase in student "fees." The subject at times was confused publicly by an asinine argument over semantics: whether to call increased charges to students "fees' or "tuition." Three years after he opened the battle for tuition, the Governor was victorious. New tuition charges of up to $600 a year more than doubled the previous "fees" for all students at the university. They are still rising.

Throughout his term, Reagan kept insisting that tuition would not impose any hardship on students and that his deep budget cuts would not really affect the quality of higher education. His euphoric logic was absurd. Somehow it could not penetrate Reagan's closed mind that hundreds of dollars in extra tuition charges meant the difference between going to college or not for thousands of students. (Two-thirds of all university students were already working in full- or part-time jobs to pay their way.) And he was simply far removed from reality to think that orders for budget cuts to 20 per cent or more would not diminish the quality of learning in the universities and colleges.

University Regent Frederick Dutton clarified some of the real effects of tuition. It would, he estimated, "trigger a major property tax increase by forcing up to 14,000 students to turn to community colleges dependent on property taxes instead of going to state colleges or the university, which rely on the state general fund."

There were other, more obvious and tragic results. Thousands of qualified, eligible students have been turned away from California's colleges in the past few years. In August 1969 the *Sacramento Bee* commented:

> In the field of higher education the Reagan program is disgraceful. California's once lauded excellence in providing opportunities for all qualified students to go to college has been diminished.
>
> The sad situation at the Sacramento State College is a case in point. SSC officials have turned away 1,125 applicants for admission this fall, . . . 85 to 95 per cent of them qualified. The rejection of these students marked the first time in the twenty-year history of the college qualified applicants were denied. . . .
>
> Compounding the picture is the fact there is no other institution of higher learning nearby that can handle the turn-aways. Only one of the eighteen state colleges is still accepting applications—in Fresno. . . .
>
> The Reagan Administration with its lack of concern for the plight of the thousands of students who cannot get into college may go down in history as the one that ruined this state's system of higher education so badly it will take years to recuperate.

In other areas of the state, the situation was worse. The *San Francisco Examiner* reported on September 29, 1969, that between 8,000 and 10,000 eligible students were turned away from San Francisco State College for that term.

The Reagan Administration argued that students turned away from one college could attend another that was less crowded, ignoring the fact that thousands of students would not be able to afford college if they had to move to another area and could not live at home. And the Board of Governors of the California Community Colleges (two-year junior colleges) declared, in September 1969, that their entire system would break down unless community college graduates could be assured of admission to state colleges.

The University of California, with nine campuses in various areas of the state, barely handled most qualified applicants. But on February 6, 1970, after Reagan cut the regents budget from $374 million to $344 million, the *San Francisco Chronicle* reported:

> University of California President Charles J. Hitch yesterday bit the bullet and said the university can live with the budget proposed by Governor Ronald Reagan. . . .
> But Hitch said the Reagan budget provides no funds "for improving existing programs, and no funds for new programs, which means that we are prevented from carrying out effectively one of our primary roles—the pursuit of new knowledge."
> Hitch noted the budget does not contain enough construction funds to meet growth demands. . . . "Last year we received less than 35 per cent of our very carefully considered capital request. This year that meager percentage has dropped to less than 20 per cent." . . .
> Hitch warned that if the situation continues over a period of years, it will be "impossible to provide facilities for all qualified students in the decade of the 1970's."

The drastic reductions of university and college budgets not only indicated Reagan's irritation with past events on the campuses; he was being blind to the future—the near future. California's total population growth has slowed in recent years, but it is still adding thousands of new citizens every year. And the part of the population that is growing at the fastest rate is the school-age group. Reagan may think that he is merely retaliating against current student "troublemakers" or trimming fiscal "fat." But the innocent are suffering now as a result of diminished quality of education in the university and college systems, and, during the next several years—at least—growing numbers of able young men and women just won't be able to get into the universities and colleges.

By contrast, one satisfaction I felt as I left the Governor's office was that from 1959 through 1966 we built three new campuses of the University of California and added eight new state colleges. Both the quality of education and the physical capacities of the campuses were keeping pace with the needs of our young people. It took money, planning, and long-range commitments to do the job.

On the issue of tuition, I know that those extra hundreds of dollars are critical to young men and women not supported by wealthy parents. My wife, Bernice, her brother, and three sisters all went to the University of California at Berkeley. They were the children of a San Francisco police captain, who earned a modest salary. Each of them lived at home and commuted—by ferry boat, streetcar, and train— every day to Berkeley for three or four years. They could not have achieved that advanced education if tuition had been charged.

My support for tuition-free higher education was strengthened on less personal grounds. The money the state spends on higher education is the best investment possible, and not just toward humanitarian goals. Every reliable survey confirms that a college education substantially boosts the income of a citizen during his lifetime. A Californian with an academic degree will earn far more money each year than one who has stopped his education after high school. And he will (with his own increasing complaints) pay more in taxes. The state, with the graduated income tax, gets back in tax revenue what it spent earlier for college and university services. The economic advantages of a sound system of higher education are diverse. In an editorial criticizing Reagan's education budget cuts, the *San Francisco Chronicle* noted: "If the university and state colleges are the primary source of leadership that brings . . . research and development funds to California, that is certainly one of the strongest reasons for the state's recognizing that its higher education system should be kept strong."

The *Chronicle* added that education and research generates more jobs (and California needs them; its unemployment rate is substantially higher than in the rest of the nation) and that about a third of the billions spent for federal research and development programs come to California. Research funds go to those places that have the talent, and California's scientific and educational talent is unsurpassed. Almost half of America's Nobel Prize winners are in California. Dr. W. K. H. Panofsky, the director of the Stanford Linear Accelerator Center (Stanford is a private university), said in 1967: "There is no doubt in my mind that the primary reason for California's leadership in scientific and technical talent lies in its state university and state colleges."

California's magnificent research resources do much more than just draw federal funds into the state. That research is constantly paying off in ways that directly improve the state's economy. California's agriculture, for example, is the most modern, efficient, and productive in the world, in large measure because of the agricultural techniques developed through research at the University of California at Davis and other campuses. Radically new and more efficient harvesting machines and farming methods created at Davis have stimulated the economy of the state and helped produce more food for a hungry nation and world.

Reagan ignored such immense benefits of the state's higher education system. One of his favorite negative platform themes was to downgrade the importance of research. The exaggerated image he drew for a suspicious public was that of an absent-minded professor who doesn't like to teach and instead sits in ivory-tower seclusion indulging his "intellectual curiosity." There are legitimate and controversial questions about the research versus teaching roles of university and college staffs, but instead of just doubting the research role and damning higher education, Reagan ought to have recognized publicly that both research and teaching are essential functions of a university. And instead of attacking a whole university and college system for the contemptuous actions of troublemakers, he should have praised the contributions of the university to California's economy, prosperity, and people.

Reagan's war against the academic community—the budget slashes, the harassment of administrators, the constant public statements downgrading research and threatening other crackdowns—halted progress in getting the best people to staff the universities and colleges. As early as the spring of 1967 the *Sacramento Bee* reported the university's increasing difficulties in the recruitment and retention of faculty. On April 12 the *Bee* reported: "The University . . . and the state college system are having more difficulty seeking faculty members than they have ever had before. At the University of California at Davis there were several men who appeared to be sure additions to the campus faculty for the 1967–68 academic year. At the last moment, they backed out and refused to sign contracts."

Reagan found new ways to wage his war on the academic community and to discourage faculty, administrators, and students. He not only was stingy on faculty salaries—sometimes vetoing legislation for promised pay raises—but also stepped perilously close to outright political control of professors on philosophical grounds.

In the spring of 1969 Reagan supported and pushed a proposal to diminish academic independence by giving the regents veto power over the hiring and firing of professors. In February a controversy developed over the rehiring at the University's San Diego campus of Dr. Herbert Marcuse, a noted Marxist philosopher and writer. In his press conference of February 25, 1969, Reagan was asked about the issue and slithered through a series of semantic evasions obscuring his basic attitude:

QUESTIONER: Governor, at the regents' meeting there was a motion made to censure Dr. McGill [chancellor] in SanDiego for his action in hiring Marcuse. How did you vote on that?

REAGAN: No, there was no move to censure. . . . We were helpless, there was nothing we could do to alter the situation with regard to Professor Marcuse—his rehiring was an accomplished fact. The regents then voted to release a statement to the press expressing their displeasure . . . that simply stated that a substantial number of regents disapproved of the action in the rehiring of Professor Marcuse. . . . A substantial number must have meant majority because it took a majority vote to approve that press statement. I voted for that press statement. . . .

QUESTIONER: Does the regents' action pretty well guarantee that [Marcuse's] contract will not be renewed next year?

REAGAN: What can happen in a year to change someone's mind—you'd have to speak to each individual. I cannot foresee anything that would change my own opinion . . . as to whether he should be there or not.

QUESTIONER: Could the Chancellor rehire him without going through the regents?

REAGAN: I have a hunch the regents will be a little more alert. As a matter of fact, we now have a motion that will be taken up at the next meeting to take the authority of chancellors to make those decisions . . . away from them and return to the regents the right to approve.

QUESTIONER: Would you support such a motion?

REAGAN: Yes, I will.

QUESTIONER: What are your reasons for your vote on the [previous] regents' action?

REAGAN: ". . . I believe there is an imbalance in the faculty of the university system, and frankly I don't believe—this isn't just a case of deciding someone's philosophy or something. I do believe that he [Marcuse] is an open advocate of the type of revolution that's causing so much disturbance in the campuses."

On April 22 Reagan was bluntly asked this question:

QUESTIONER: Governor, on the subject of the Board of
    Regents taking over the hiring at the University of
    California . . . you say political philosophy will not
    enter into the decision. What other than political
    philosophy are the regents competent to judge a man
    by as to whether he should or shouldn't teach?
REAGAN: This question has come up before as to whether
    the regents are competent to make these decisions or
    not and I challenge the assumption that in the whole
    United States and in all of government and
    everything the only facet of government that should
    be allowed to run itself without any public control
    whatsoever is in the educational field. . . .
QUESTIONER: . . . Mr. [William] Roth, who is one of the
    regents, said he's never known of any instance where a
    regent has considered a faculty appointment that
    hasn't been on a political basis. . . .
REAGAN: . . . Mr. Roth is distorting the situation. . . . I never
    heard of anyone on our side . . . opposed to a faculty
    member bringing up his politics as a reason.
QUESTIONER: Well, could you explain then, Governor, you
    once talked about the controversy over Professor
    Marcuse . . . and you've said he represented a political
    imbalance in the system. . . .
REAGAN: He's in one of the inexact sciences, philosophy,
    to be exact, and the thing . . . is not so much the views
    of an individual as the lack of competency when an
    individual reveals that he injects his own views in
    his teaching.

The Governor's war against higher education sank to a
low and despicable level when Robert F. Kennedy was assassinated in Los Angeles in June 1968. In a letter to college
trustees and university regents, mailed the day after the

Senator's death, Reagan linked the murder to "today's climate of violence."

"A sick campus community in California in many ways is responsible for a sick community around these campuses," Reagan wrote. His letter, made public, continued: "It is time for [trustees and regents] to reassess their own goals, their pattern of only reacting to crisis, meeting by meeting, and the degree to which they have delegated away responsibility and abandoned principle." The letter questioned "constant resistance" by some professors and administrators to "the rightful place of law enforcement in a democratic society," then concluded: "Do you think that constant appeasement of those who coerce . . . is likely to strengthen confidence in society, in leadership, in fair play?"

Reagan's sense of "fair play" in relation to the university regents seemed to vary, depending on whether or not they agreed with him. He was publicly pleased about the regents and defended their "competence" when they voted with him on the issue of veto power over the hiring and firing of faculty. But when the regents turned down, 13 to 8, a motion by Reagan to sweep away such faculty prerogatives as establishment and supervision of courses, the Governor blew up. On October 21, 1968, he accused the regents of "disdain and deliberate unconcern for the interests of the people."

The Governor's anti-education policies toward public schools below the university and college level have been only slightly less destructive than his war on higher education. In early 1968 Milton L. Schwartz, outgoing vice president of the State Board of Education, said, in a farewell statement, that Reagan was "the greatest destructive force and enemy of public education in fifty years." Schwartz, a Republican, said that 1967 was "a black, black page in the history of public education. In previous years, we made progress, but last year public education moved at a dizzy pace in a backward direction." He listed these actions on various school measures:

- a bill to provide funds to train teachers of disadvantaged children—cut one-third by Reagan
- a bill to help gifted children of disadvantaged families—vetoed by Reagan
- a bill to provide college education grants to poverty area children—vetoed by Reagan
- a bill to raise the minimum salaries of teachers in California to $6,000 a year—vetoed by Reagan

Schwartz was angry, a typical reaction to Reagan's negative policies and actions on education. "You can't justify these things on the grounds of fiscal responsibility and economy," the education leader said. "These measures and others like them were passed by the legislature. But the Governor is willing to sign a bill giving property tax relief of $5 million to oil companies."

One fleeting hint of a change of heart in the Reagan war against higher education came in a statement in March by the Governor's finance director, Verne Orr. At the beginning of a speech to the California Taxpayers Association in San Francisco, the Reagan finance director blithely boasted that the university and college budgets had increased in four years and proclaimed: "There is not one area in which the Reagan Administration has been more fair, generous, and liberal than in higher education." (I'm glad I wasn't there; I would have either burst out laughing or fallen out of my chair.) Orr's perverted claim of charity toward higher education, of course, was based on the misleading, narrow fact that the budget had increased. It was bound to because of rising enrollments and inflation. He did not mention that, a month before, Reagan had chopped the university regents' budget request by $41 million.

However shallow the pretense of charity toward higher education, it lasted only a moment. Before Orr's speech was over, he was attacking college and university administrators for their complaints about budget slashes, charging that they "are failing to turn out a salable product" and warning ominously that the higher education system might "have to find new administrators."

It is a tribute to the university that it survived the Reagan years only slightly tarnished and diminished in stature. Nobody knows how many outstanding scholars may have elected to go elsewhere rather than accept appointment to a university faculty or staff with such a rabid enemy in the highest office in the state, but it is safe to assume that a substantial number did just that.

Continuing if diminishing growth of California, plus the determined efforts of enlightened legislators of both parties, blocked Reagan's most destructive sallies against funding for the institutions. An alert press made it plain that Reagan's attacks were ill-conceived and his attempts to starve the university and college systems were dangerous, counterproductive actions.

Without these restraints, this man who "still puddles up when he hears the Eureka alma mater" may very well have destroyed what most experts concede to be the greatest public system of higher education on earth. One wonders who such a man would appoint as Secretary of Health, Education, and Welfare and what the appointee's mandate might be. Reagan played a role in sending Casper W. Weinberger to Washington in the dying days of the Nixon administration. As Secretary of HEW, Weinberger quickly earned the nickname "Cap the Knife" for his ruthless slashing away at both budgets and programs. And in his ill-conceived $90 billion tax saving scheme Reagan would turn most educational programs over to the states, thus ending the federal guidelines that have helped ensure equal opportunity for all Americans in the quest for education and the chance to rise to higher station.

As for campus turmoil, it continued in California and across not only the United States but the rest of the free world as long as the Vietnam War continued and as long as students felt compelled to take to the streets to redress grievances. I deplore violence, always have. I prefer negotiation to confrontation. Nevertheless, when the Berkeley problem escalated in 1964 I moved quickly to restore order and was sharply criticized by many friends for calling in the police to calm the campus. But in the darkest days it would never occur to me to exact retribution from the university system. That does not seem to me to be the action of a reasonable man.

6
Quick-Draw Justice

Western history buffs know that Roy Bean was "the law west of the Pecos," and anyone who appeared before Bean was lucky to escape with his life. There is no recorded case in which an offender hauled into Bean's drumhead court got out without at least being divested of all his possessions—and that was punishment for milder offenses. Since most offenders wound up on the gallows and the rest on a rail headed out of town, it is safe to assume that the recidivism rate was low indeed in Langtry, Texas, His Honor's wholly owned town.

Ronald Reagan never had a chance to play Judge Bean in the movies, but he has been doing his best to emulate him in real life for the past ten years. An ardent law and order advocate, Reagan placed emphasis on crime and violence as the main election issue in his gubernatorial campaigns. Crime is, indeed, a pervasive problem in modern society and an important, legitimate subject for public discussion. But Reagan's treatment of crime as an issue was narrowly political and dangerously misleading. He spent more time thrashing the already growing public fear about crime and

violence than on calm attempts to place the issue in a
rational perspective. His speeches not only dramatized the
growing incidence of crime in California; they sen-
sationalized it. Reagan's receptive audiences heard innumerable gory and garish descriptions of crime, which
fortified their notions that "law and order" had broken
down and that it was no longer safe to walk the streets of any
city at any hour. The courts, particularly the Supreme Court,
were "coddling criminals" through decisions guaranteeing
Constitutional rights; Democrats, particularly incumbent
Democratic leaders, were "soft on crime." Reagan encouraged his listeners to be both judge and jury. That civil
liberties were part of every American's Constitutional
inheritance or that crucial differences existed between
individual crimes of violence and collective civil disobedience were basic democratic ideas lost on him.

Reagan's approach to the ancient, complex, and human
problem of crime and violence was and is characteristically
negative and simplistic. Aside from his occasional
statements of vague "objectives" and meager, nonfunded
legislative programs, he concentrated while Governor on a
single solution to crime: tougher punishment for the
criminal. In Reagan's narrow view, that meant less
discretion for the courts and longer prison sentences for the
convicted. Swift and harsh punishment, he firmly believes
and constantly makes clear, is the prime "deterrent" to
crime.

Every thinking political leader is appalled by crime rates,
which continue to rise. But most know that there is a
combination of circumstances involved and that the
problem does not lend itself to simplistic, single-barrel
solution.

There is widespread agreement among penologists that
mandatory sentences are a crippling blow against the
laudable aim of society to rehabilitate first offenders.
Further, judges are robbed of discretion under mandatory
sentencing laws; no matter how mitigating the cir-

cumstances or how repentant and deserving the defendant may seem to be, the judge has no options. One must wonder whether the goal of keeping hardened criminals off the streets longer is worth risking an enormous increase in prison populations because of "hard time" sentences for many first offenders who conceivably could be returned to a useful and productive life if judicial discretion were allowed.

Reagan shows some ambivalence from time to time, but he always returns to his medieval notion of locking offenders up for longer and longer periods as the best answer. As an example of vintage Reagan, here's part of what he told the National Sheriffs Association in a speech shortly after he became governor. As usual, he began with humorous references to his days in motion pictures:

> First time I ever played a sheriff, the director told me all I had to have was a hard head and a white hat. I think your job takes a little more than that. But I'm sure most of you agree that what is needed more than anything in our country today is people with a hard-headed approach to our problems and a vital interest in seeing them solved.
>
> This is especially true in the field of law enforcement, where the problems increase daily and where there are no easy solutions. I once played a sheriff who thought he could do the job without a gun. I was dead in twenty-seven minutes of a thirty minute show. You may still have your guns, but there are those who've done everything but tie your hands and take your guns. It is time for society to give those on the firing line the weapons they need in the fight against crime.

In that speech, Reagan proceeded to discuss—with diminishing humor—the basic and urgent problem of crime and violence in America. It was a tough, "hard-headed" speech, which established the basic themes he repeated throughout his terms as Governor.

He laid the blame for increasing crime rates to almost everything from the permissive attitude of parents to the restrictions of child labor laws, with heavy and indignant emphasis on "court decisions which have narrowed the difference between liberty and license." He minimized the factor of poverty as one cause of crime and mocked "the theory that says society is to blame." But as a former motion picture and television actor, he neglected to mention the screen's glorification of violence as a factor contributing to modern crime.

In his remarks to the Sheriffs Association and in most of his later speeches on crime, Reagan spoke far more vaguely about the solutions to the problem of crime than about the causes. "We have four main objectives," he said. "First, to provide statewide planning and for orderly and effective development in the field of criminal justice. Second, we wish to expect to maintain the traditional partnership and cooperation between the agencies of state and local government. Third, we must provide coordination of those agencies and groups involved in criminal justice projects. Fourth, we must provide a vehicle to handle federal-state relations, and to implement federal legislation dealing with crime control." Those statements are devoid of meaning.

Reagan's "objectives" were a faint echo of his decisive campaign pledges to crack down on crime. "Planning . . . cooperation . . . coordination . . . implementation"? Those are commendable concepts, of course, but imprecise. In a remarkably short time after settling in Sacramento, Reagan was beginning to sound amazingly like the politicians he had for so long denounced. His promised crusade against crime lacked that one vital element that any increased law enforcement effort would require: money. The Governor's economy gospel apparently took priority even over his zealous campaign pledges to reduce crime in California.

I do not know of a single state in the Union that has adequate prison facilities for today's inmate population, let alone a quantum jump such as would follow the imposition of harsh mandatory sentence laws. To construct the needed facilities, all of the maximum security variety, would have

cost hundreds and hundreds of millions of dollars. Reagan
and others who sang their simplistic little ditty about "let the
punishment fit the crime" failed to inform their audiences of
many of these hard facts.

So even the one toughly specific anticrime measure by
Reagan—longer prison terms for some criminals—seemed a
bit shaky in light of his blanket order for budget cuts in all
state operations. Two months after he proposed legislation
to lengthen prison terms for some crimes, his staff
announced that the State Department of Corrections would
lose 140 employees as a result of his orders to economize.
Significantly, all officials of the state's prisons and other
correctional facilities were instructed not to discuss their
new budgets with "outsiders."

The emphasis Reagan gives to punishment and longer
prison sentences as deterrents to crime is not matched by his
attention to improving California's prison facilities. In 1970
the *San Francisco Examiner* published a series of articles
reporting on increasing violence and other troubles in the
state's prisons. In reaction to the series, former State Director
of Corrections Richard McGee said that the major state
prisons at San Quentin and Folsom were "obsolete" and
definitely "not the answer" to the problem of dealing with
convicted criminals. Roy K. Procunier, Director of Corrections under Reagan, commented:

> For the relatively few serious troublemakers we have no
> better answer than bars and walls and strong sur-
> veillance. For the great majority of prisoners, though,
> we can offer a measure of hope and a chance for a better
> life. We try very hard to do this, even in outdated plants
> like Quentin and Folsom. We could do a better job if all
> prisons were small and modern, but it would cost an
> enormous amount of money.

Another glaring contradiction between Reagan's promise
and performance in crime control came on the "pre-
emption" issue. He had stated repeatedly during the

campaign that the state should not "pre-empt" the ability of local governments to adopt local laws relating to crime. He blithely abandoned the "pre-emption" concept when his right-wing attitudes surged to the surface on one controversial issue: gun control. Reagan opposed steps by San Francisco and Beverly Hills to establish modest local control over registration of handguns, and he even pushed for state legislation to prohibit cities or counties from adopting such ordinances. The Governor forgot his lofty ideas about "pre-emption" and used language strikingly similar to the propaganda of such groups as the National Rifle Association and the John Birch Society. "People kill people; guns don't kill them," he said. Recent public opinion surveys show that 70 per cent of Americans favor control of handguns, but Reagan has not moderated his views on this important question.

I hesitate even now to use the scary statistics of rising crime rates, because they are, by themselves, misleading and confusing. There is no longer any question that crime, and particularly violent crime, is rising throughout the nation. Crime in California according to FBI statistics *increased* in all categories during the years 1966–74, the full term of Reagan's Governorship. Population rose by more than 2 million or about 15 per cent during that period—but crime increased much more dramatically: Murder rose 115 per cent; forcible rape, 98 per cent; robberies, 130 per cent. The dreary, depressing statistics continue through a long series of crimes against both person and property. Everywhere the story is the same: Crime in California rose 100 per cent or more during Reagan's years as Governor.

Let me make it clear that I do not hold Reagan responsible for the increases, nor am I unmindful of the fact that there were similar and sometimes even greater increases in other states. New York, for example, shows corresponding or greater percentage increases even though the population of that state remained virtually constant during the period of the study. My purpose in reciting these statistics is to illuminate the difference between Reagan's self-serving and simplistic pronouncements and the actual trend of events. Crime was climbing steadily upward during all those years of Reagan's harsh rhetoric about law and order. He apparently failed to realize that there was no simple solution to the problem or that his inflammatory remarks were doing nothing to solve matters. It is this tendency to ignore facts and continue to preach the same old creed that I find most dangerous in the man.

In his efforts to justify his lack of action to fight poverty, Reagan is fond of quoting partial statistics indicating that crime increased less sharply during the Depression than during the times of prosperity. But there is no question that poverty, as well as such related factors as high unemployment and deplorable living conditions, does substantially contribute to rising crime rates, particularly when that poverty is concentrated in ghettos in the midst of affluence. Expert studies have confirmed that the highest incidence of crime is among those groups in our population whose recent expectations for progress in their lives have been frustrated. The tremendous migration of minority citizens and the rural poor to California in recent decades has been a major factor in California's higher crime rates. They came to the "Golden State" expecting immediate and substantial improvement in their lives. The frustration of those hopes, through racial discrimination and other conditions, led to despair for many and crime for some. Studies of criminal statistics also indicate that crime is particularly high in areas of transient population. The frequent movement of people within California adds to its high crime rate.

The prevention of crime is a massive challenge, requiring varied steps by society and government to improve the conditions of life for our most impoverished and desperate citizens. The control of crime is still a demanding challenge, but the essential need, I feel, is relatively obvious: more police and more modern police methods. To reduce the soaring crime rates, governments must move to place more policemen in the high-crime neighborhoods of our cities and communities. And they must move to improve the quality of police departments. That means higher salaries for policemen, better communications equipment, and more sophisticated training and techniques in crime control. Such steps require leadership at the highest political levels—and money. Reagan provided neither; he was content to offer the people only an angry, louder echo of their fears.

And, once the campaign was over and Reagan no longer felt compelled to continue his "soft on crime" charges against me, he played a different tune. A few weeks after he became Governor, he told a gathering of the state's law officers that "California is fortunate to have the best law enforcement to be found anywhere in the world."

As Governor, Reagan continued to damn and denounce the courts with almost as much fervor as expressed by Alabama's George Wallace. There is an ironic contradiction apparent in Reagan's "law and order" attitudes, which was noted in a reporter's question during a 1968 press conference:

QUESTIONER: Governor, . . . during the past year you've been highly critical of some of the statements of the courts, including the California Supreme Court, which you consider to be beyond the boundary of propriety. At the same time you condemn—rather, refuted—those who choose to disobey laws that they find immoral. Is there some inconsistency here? Some people have criticized you as a person who wants to uphold law for others, but who will readily dissent from a court decision if it goes against you.

REAGAN: No, as a matter of fact, I've never advocated dissenting from a court or not upholding a court opinion. . . .

The Governor added in that answer that he had a right to "criticize" court decisions. But he neglected to mention the vitriolic tone of so many statements in which he had impugned the integrity of respected judges and justices. Frequently, Reagan angrily denounced the courts and specific court decisions almost in the same breath as he complained that public respect for the law was breaking down. In early 1970 a Los Angeles judge completed an exhaustive legal study of school segregation in the area and issued a lengthy, carefully written decision ordering school integration there on Constitutional grounds. Reagan, hotly contentious in the midst of a controversy over the school busing issue, condemned that judge's decision as "ridiculous."

Most often, his wrath has been aroused by court decisions protecting the Constitutional rights of individuals accused of or arrested for crime. His phrasing in such denouncements usually leaves the impression that he believes the courts are in some sort of conspiratorial alliance with the criminal elements of society, not only condoning but encouraging crime. It is another irony of the Reagan record that he, like so many right-wing conservatives, is constantly lauding the United States Constitution as a brilliant document of law but also constantly denouncing the specific application of the Bill of Rights and other provisions of the Constitution to protect contemporary citizens from the abuses of authority.

Other societies have different attitudes about safeguarding the rights of all citizens and protecting the innocent. Under the Hispanic system of jurisprudence there is no presumption of innocence, rather the reverse, as many Americans learn to their sorrow when they become involved with the law in Mexico and are dispatched to jail with nothing like due process of law as we understand it. The dictatorships of the world, whether they are of the right or the left, show little respect for the rights of citizens; witness the incarceration of authors in the Soviet Union or "enemies of the state" in Greece under the colonels or Spain under Franco.

There is, of course, a price exacted for this peculiarly American concern, but it is a price most of us pay willingly.

Protection of the innocent from a wrathful or dictatorial system of justice and careful preservation of the liberties we cherish so much is an eminently worthwhile objective.

In the area of civil liberties—the rights of the individual guaranteed by the Constitution—Reagan's attitudes seem to stem more from the values of the Middle Ages than even the mood of the Old West. For example, in March 1970 a United Press International reporter from Los Angeles was arrested in Santa Barbara while he was officially covering student disturbances near the University of California campus there. The reporter, Stewart Slavin, showed police his valid press credentials, but he was handcuffed and then jailed for twenty hours and told that he was charged with "curfew violation" and that bail would be $1,250. During the twenty hours he was denied permission to make a phone call to his office, family, or legal counsel. Slavin was later released and the charge was dropped, but UPI President Mims Thomason protested in a letter to Reagan "the utter disregard shown by law enforcement authorities in Santa Barbara . . . to the professional and personal rights of a United Press International correspondent." When Reagan was asked to comment on the violation of the reporter's civil liberties, he responded, "He should be happy he was captured by the good guys."

The Santa Barbara disturbance at which Slavin was arrested was only one event in the turmoil that churned through the nation's college campuses in recent years. The first major campus disorder struck at the University of California at Berkeley in 1964 and became a political issue that Ronald Reagan rode with great skill and obvious relish in his first campaign for Governor. His stern rhetoric fell on fertile ground; many or perhaps most Californians were confused, frightened, angered, and alienated by the, to them, pointless demonstrations, which at least once threatened to shut down the state's great university system. As far as can be ascertained, Reagan's views remain unchanged, and it seems likely that substantial numbers of people remain alienated

by the campus uprisings, even though they have now largely
subsided (perhaps because of today's faltering economy or,
more likely in my opinion, because the end of the Vietnam
War removed the major cause for the conflict).

The Berkeley issue was one of the main factors in my
defeat by Reagan in the gubernatorial election of 1966. As a
candidate, I was caught in the same political vise that
squeezed many moderate or liberal incumbents out of office.
The growing number of indignant conservatives in the state
were against me because I had not appeared to be tough
enough in cracking down on student disorder during the
Free Speech Movement. The ultraliberals and more militant
allies of the students were against me because I had called out
extra police to end the sit-ins. It was one example of the
dilemma continually faced by the moderate political leader
who seeks to conciliate among warring factions.

> The National Commission on the Causes and
> Prevention of Violence reported: The problem of
> campus unrest is more than a campus problem. There
> is no single cause, no single solution. We urge all
> Americans to reject hasty and simplistic answers. We
> urge them to distinguish between peaceful protest and
> violent disruption, between the nonconformity of
> youth and the terror tactics of the extremists. . . .
> Although much of the discontent often focuses on
> grievances within the campus environment, it is rooted
> in dissatisfactions with the larger society. . . .
> Students are unwilling to accept the gaps between
> professed ideals and actual performance. They see
> afresh the injustices that remain unremedied. . . .
> Today's intelligent, idealistic students see a nation
> which has achieved the physical ability to provide food,
> shelter, and education for all, but has not yet devised
> social institutions that do so. They see a society, built
> on the principle that all men are created equal, that has
> not yet assured equal opportunity in life. They see a
> world of nation-states with the technical brilliance to

harness the ultimate energy but without the common sense to agree on methods of preventing mutual destruction.

To cope with such strong feeling, particularly to deal firmly with nihilistic minorities who take advantage of others' legitimate grievances to embark on a course of violent disruption, is a task that challenges the intelligence and cool-headedness of any public official faced with it.

Reagan, as a gubernatorial candidate in 1966, was not caught in the dilemma. He gave the angry majority what it wanted: an angry voice speaking for authority and order and against the troublesome students. Reagan simply picked sides in the conflict and, despite an occasional vague disclaimer, made it clear to the public that he would crack down on student dissidents. He added his own special touches in the campaign of 1966: the charges that I was "soft" on student disorder; that university faculty members were often lazy, research-preoccupied agitators; and that university administrators were vacillating appeasers. Above all, he left voters with the unqualified impression that he would stop what he repeatedly called "mob violence."

For a while after his inauguration, Reagan still insisted—in general terms—that he would stop campus disorders. In a November 1967 speech in Anaheim, the Governor pledged that his administration stood "ready to move at a moment's notice to stop riots before they start." The principal function of government, he declared, "is to protect society from the lawbreaker."

But the war on the state's campuses expanded. Berkeley barely got its breath back after the end of one crisis when another erupted. San Francisco State College was torn by an almost uninterrupted series of disorders. As one campus temporarily cooled, another burst into turmoil. The war moved to San José State College, to the University of California at Los Angeles, to San Diego State College. The sequence of disturbances reached tragic proportions with the

People's Park battle at Berkeley in the spring of 1969 (one dead, more than two hundred injured) and the riots at Santa Barbara in early 1970 (millions of dollars of damage to local businesses).

Logically and politically, Reagan by all odds should have been in a tough and difficult spot. He had won election, in part, by exploiting public impatience over a single major campus disturbance during my administration, the Free Speech Movement trouble at Berkeley. He had pledged to crack down on student disorders and stop the campus turmoil. But, faced by a rising wave of campus turmoil during his administration, Reagan saw the light—and apparently had finally read the state Constitution. Except for the appointment of regents and his own membership on that board, the Governor of California is prohibited from any direct involvement in the operation of state universities and colleges. His only formal authority related to a campus disorder is to call out state police or the National Guard— but only when the help is requested by local officials. Reagan did this often and eagerly as Governor, as the campus war escalated beyond the capacities of college and local law enforcement personnel. His political strategy was simple. He abandoned the shaky reasoning of 1966 that placed responsibility for campus peace in the lap of the Governor. As Governor, his reasoning found a new scapegoat for the war on the campuses: university administrators. As he explained in December 1967, while San Francisco State College was in turmoil, "In this state more than any other state that I know of, there are great restrictions as to what the governmental authorities can do."

But a Governor does have, beyond his limited legal authority, immense influence of an informal sort. The effect of his voice and words, as the highest elected official of the state, is powerful, particularly on an issue as controversial and emotional as campus turmoil. In the passions of student discontent, radical agitation, and public impatience, the

temper and tone of the Governor's statements can be
critically influential.

In effect, Reagan declared and sustained verbal warfare
against the entire academic community of California: the
student "mob," the "agitating" professors, the "vacillating"
administrators, and the "appeasing" chancellors. His
denunciations were invariably generalized. When challeng-
ed by reporters to identify actual examples of "appeasement"
or individual "vacillating" administrators, he would weasel
away from "specifics." Occasionally, he would speak
magnanimously about the majority of "responsible and
orderly" students and professors, but so parenthetically and
so briefly that the comments seldom gained much public
attention. Reagan is perceptive enough about the workings
of the news media to know that his blanket, angry
condemnations—not his mild, occasional disclaimers—
would get the headlines and public attention. The total
effect of his public rhetoric and propaganda on campus
disorders, as on so many other issues, was to plant the
simplistic good guys–bad guys theme on the public
consciousness, thus adding fuel to the fiery passions on
the campuses.

His rigid stance, his simplistic instinct to join one side of a
conflict, was unwavering during the People's Park battle in
Berkeley. There was no question that the controversy
stemming from the use of a university-owned vacant lot by
Berkeley "street people" and students as a park escalated
into violence as the result of mistakes, confusion, and
intransigence on all sides. Some nihilistic agitators abused
the People's Park issue as a pretext for confrontation with
authorities. Some of the young people taunted police, and a
few broke windows in the area and threw bricks at sheriff's
deputies. University officials and civic authorities misjudg-
ed the tense situation and failed to find a solution. But it was
also starkly evident that law enforcement personnel often
acted with excessive and unjustified brutality. Mayor Joseph

Alioto of San Francisco, who had helped resolve one crisis at San Francisco State College with the measured and restrained use of police, labeled the performance of the law enforcement personnel on the People's Park battle as "amateur night in Berkeley." The indiscriminate use of shotguns (with both birdshot and buckshot) resulted in death for one man, blindness for another, and dozens of serious injuries. For the first time in American history, a state conducted an aerial attack on civilians when a sheriff's officer sent a National Guard helicopter over the campus to spew tear gas. The gas sickened and terrified not only student demonstrators but also university employees and patients in a nearby hospital. The sloppy roundup and arrests of several hundred young people—and their subsequent mistreatment at a nearby detention center—resulted a year later in federal indictments against several sheriff's deputies.

How did Reagan react? He continued, in broad generalities, to condemn "the mob" of students and defended the law enforcement personnel. The blatantly brutal tactics of some sheriff's officers, the death of a young man, the gas-spewing helicopter? He shrugged them off without comment or a "that's-the-way-the-ball-bounces-in-war" remark.

The critical judgment of police tactics during the People's Park battle is not just my own. On May 30 the *Los Angeles Times* said in an editorial: "They played into the hands of the revolutionaries by a use of repressive force beyond any order of magnitude required. As a result, those whom the law was supposed to protect were given cause to distrust and fear the law."

The *Sacramento Bee* was particularly angered by the mass arrests during the battle. It commented on July 11: "So methodical was the herding of a crowd into a closed area that it appeared to be planned repression rather than on-the-spot enforcement of the law. The aftermath of this military exercise now discloses how inept and unnecessary was the tactic. All 416 of the mass arrest cases have been dismissed in court."

Such developments, I am convinced, were the result, in part, of Reagan's jingoistic, shoot-from-the-hip "law and order" rhetoric.

Reagan's reaction to the various demonstrations against Vietnam War policies in recent years is reminiscent of the hysteria of the Joseph McCarthy era in the early 1950s. Those demonstrations, sometimes bursting into violence but most often peaceful, elicited contempt from Reagan. In October 1967 he said that Communists were spurring the antiwar demonstrations that were beginning to sweep across the United States and several other nations. Ragan said in Des Moines, Iowa, "We'd be pretty naïve to rule out the part Communists play in these demonstrations." In the same month and in other speeches, the Governor clearly alleged "treason" in antiwar demonstrations and then—in irresponsible indifference to several delicate questions of international law and diplomacy—said: "There would be plenty of laws to cover them [the demonstrators] if we were technically in a state of war." Pressed by reporters, Reagan stopped short of urging a declaration of war against North Vietnam (he did later in a different context) but suggested that it might be possible to "implement the same rules" against antiwar protestors. Backed into a logical corner, he did finally acknowledge that such "treason" laws and rules should not be applied to peaceful demonstrators.

On such issues Reagan not only ventured ignorantly into the legal realm but also demagogically delved into the emotions of the public. On October 26, 1967, he said: "I don't think the American people can continue to buy their sons' being asked to fight and die while that same government defends the right of the dissenter to take his dissent into actually aiding the enemy that's trying to kill their sons."

Contrary to the admonition of the Eisenhower Commission on violence, Reagan seldom made any attempt to "distinguish between peaceful protest and violent disruption, between the nonconformity of youth and the terror tactics of extremists." He angrily condemned antiwar demonstrators at the Oakland Induction Center in the fall of 1967 but made no distinction between those few who precipitated violence and the thousands who earlier assembled there peacefully, legally, and nonviolently. During the People's Park conflict he denounced those students who used violent tactics, which was understandable, but also continually condemned "the mob" of student demonstrators, which was inflammatory. He refused to give any credit at all to the tens of thousands of students, other young people, and Berkeley area residents who expressed their sympathy for People's Park in peaceful demonstrations. On Memorial Day, 1969, a crowd estimated at 50,000 marched in silent, peaceful protest against the excesses of police tactics or in support of the People's Park project. Their leaders worked with city officials and received authorization for the march and also organized teams of monitors to discourage any violence-advocating troublemakers among the throng. In a tense and volatile atmosphere, those tens of thousands of people marched several miles through Berkeley's narrow streets without a single incident of trouble. Reagan was asked about that peaceful demonstration at his press conference of June 3:

> QUESTIONER: Does the size and makeup of the demonstration in Berkeley last Friday give you any second thoughts about the size and makeup of the so-called dissident minority, which you say is challenging the university?
>
> REAGAN: No, not at all. These people have been very successful in their efforts always to cloud an issue and to try to get some innocent people involved who would not understand what was really at stake. . . . There is no question but that there are a large number

of people who misunderstood. . . . I don't blame the
kids for getting confused, for joining in a parade of
the kind that was held last Friday.

Reagan condemned and denounced "the mob" of students
for lawless or violent tactics. But when vast numbers of
students and others used legal and peaceful means of
expressing themselves they were, at best, "confused," in the
Governor's judgment. He acknowledged no "legitimate
grievance" by students on a specific issue that led to conflict.
He left no logical alternative to the student who wanted to be
heard but did not want to engage in violent tactics.

This is all doubly strange to those who have read Reagan's
autobiography, *Where's the Rest of Me?* In the book he
recalls that he rallied student strikers at Eureka to force the
resignation of a college president who had threatened to
chop so many classes as an economy move that the academic
standing of the college was threatened and some students
would not have been able to graduate. In his words, recalling
that experience, Reagan wrote: "We students found we had
achieved a lot more personal attention, plus an education in
human nature and the rights of man to universal education
that nothing could erase from our psyches."

Well, "almost nothing" might be more accurate. This
glowing memory of his own student triumph was far from
his thoughts, let alone his psyche, when he railed so
viciously against other students whose protest was, to them,
just as valid as Reagan's was to him that day long ago at
Eureka.

In his simplistic and angry statements on crime and
lawlessness, Reagan's greatest disservice has been to blur the
distinctions between the hard-core, incorrigible criminal
and the amateur, one-time law violator; between individual
crimes of violence and collective civil disobedience or, even,
peaceful demonstrations. The people need to be aware of
those distinctions and to understand the different causes and

types of crime and turmoil in our changing society. Reagan, however, obscures the differences and diminishes understanding by his blanket indictment of almost any form of crime, disorder, and staged dissent as "lawlessness on the streets."

I share the common hope that we can turn the corner against crime. I deplore the rising rates of violent crime, especially among juveniles, and the frightening recent increase in crimes by females. But I am not willing to shelve the Constitution and turn our delicately balanced system of jurisprudence into a massive kangaroo court in the process. I would hope that perceptive Americans will understand Reagan's tumultuous tirades for what they are, sound and fury, signifying nothing but a crass attempt to curry favor with the voter.

Reagan speaks often about the nobility of "freedom" and "liberty," but I doubt that he has any pragmatic conception of those worthy human conditions in today's complex society. The best answer to the Reagan mentality in today's politics—and the best warning to a fearful and confused society—is summed up by this favorite quote of mine from George Bernard Shaw:

> It is quite useless to declare that all men are born free if you deny that they are born good. Guarantee a man's goodness and his liberty will take care of itself. To guarantee his freedom on condition that you approve his moral character is formally to abolish all freedom whatsoever, as every man's liberty is at the mercy of a moral indictment which any fool can trump up against everyone who violates custom, whether as a prophet or a rascal. This is the lesson democracy has to learn before it can become anything but the most oppressive of all the priesthoods.

7
The Dark Side of
Mr. Good Guy

In his films Ronald Reagan was always the good guy. It is an image he carried over into public life and would like to project to this day.

There is a darker side to Ronald Reagan, but he doesn't talk about that. Suggest that he lacks compassion, and he tosses you a one-liner, usually something about "bleeding hearts." In Reagan's lexicon, a bleeding heart apparently is anyone who doesn't put the dollar above everything else, even above the lives of genuine unfortunates. I thank God that few people share his darkest views.

Despite ever increasing budgets and tax loads during his eight years in Sacramento, Reagan continually proclaimed himself the cut, squeeze, and trim champion. As we have already seen, his budget-slashing seriously handicapped the operations of the state university system and the rehabilitative efforts in the state's prisons. Let us now examine the efforts launched in each of his terms to cut the ground out from under California's most helpless citizens—the mentally ill, the retarded, the poverty-stricken. And let us ask ourselves, who would want to be champion of that?

One of Reagan's greatest disasters was his attempted
scuttling of California's mental health program. In
Reagan's own words: "The best hatchet job they can do on
me is in mental health." He was right, of course. The
spectacle of Mr. Nice Guy drawing down on the mental
retardates, the temporarily disaffected and disoriented, and
the hopelessly insane is not a pretty picture.

For some years now a mercifully small but very vocal
minority of the far right has been convinced that the
government effort to improve mental health is a plot,
probably Communist, to gain control over the minds of
Americans. Adherents of this paranoid notion actually
believed in the existence of a secret plot to incarcerate
hundreds of thousands of American citizens in Alaska under
the pretense that they were mentally ill. I have thought of
this extraordinary extension of the conspiracy notion for
years and pondered how such a charge could be answered
except by saying, simply, "nonsense." I have not developed a
better answer.

It would be impossible to prove that these misguided
people are all supporters of Reagan, but it seems highly
likely that many of them voted for him. If he had been elected
to do their bidding he could scarcely have found a way to
please them more than he did with his first major move as
Governor. Just two months after he took office, Reagan
abruptly announced an "economy" move to chop apart the
state's mental health program, which had been widely
recognized as the most efficient, modern, and humane of all
state programs in the nation. In his fanatical, simplistic
approach to economy, a hatchet would have been too
delicate an instrument for the new Governor. He picked up a
giant ax and swung away at California's mental health
programs with about as much precision and compassion as a
berserk Paul Bunyan.

Reagan's arbitrary fiscal attack on the state's services for
the mentally ill and the mentally retarded was a major part of

a broader "economy" crusade. Soon after his inauguration in January 1967 the Governor announced that he was ordering a flat 10 per cent reduction of the budgets of all state agencies and departments. In mid-March he grandly boasted that he would eliminate more than 4,000 state jobs within fifteen months. A few days later, one of his staff assistants disclosed that 3,700 of those jobs would come out of the State Department of Mental Hygiene. The drastic cutback of mental health personnel, they said, would save the taxpayers $17.7 million a year.

Reagan used a simple and narrow deduction to justify the huge cut in the Department of Mental Hygiene's budget. In 1959 there were 37,500 patients in California's hospitals for the mentally ill. In 1967 the number had dropped to 22,000. Using all the fiscal sophistication of a grammar school arithmetic primer, Reagan decided that with fewer patients the mental health program could be substantially reduced.

His administration ignored two basic facts relating to the financial needs of California's mental health programs. First, the number of individuals requiring attention and treatment in mental health facilities was continuing to rise, along with California's population. Although the number of institutionalized, full-time patients was decreasing, admissions were increasing. Second, the modern techniques and methods that had freed thousands of individuals from full-time institutional care remained expensive; along with everything else in an inflationary economy, the costs of effective treatment were rising.

Reagan's attempts toward drastic reductions of the state's mental health budgets was a tragedy of political callousness toward human suffering. No one will ever know, nor can anyone ever measure, the harm done to human lives as a result of the Reagan ax-wielding on mental health budgets. As a result of outrage and pressure by mental health professionals, the legislature, and the public, some of the budget cuts ordered by Reagan were later rescinded. But, at the very least, the confusion created by his careless or cynical policies set the California mental health program back several years.

One of my proudest achievements as Governor of California from 1959 to 1967 was the expansion and modernization of the state's mental health services. The breakthroughs made in this period pulled California away from the old custodial approach to the mentally incapacitated and into a new program, which achieved number one ranking from national psychiatric and public health professionals.

Under the forceful leadership of Dr. Dan Blaine, the state's mental institutions ceased being brutalizing warehouses of the insane; money formerly spent to build more and more "bughouses" was spent instead on modern drug therapies and more and better-trained personnel. Within a few years thousands of patients who had been regarded as incurably ill were released or on the road to recovery. Lives were being saved. And, in retrospect, it is fair to say that Blaine's program was the best kind of economy in government. In its first year, for example, we did add $3 million to the mental hygiene budget to pay for his modern techniques, new drugs, and trained personnel. But we also saved $3 million in that one year by not building a new $6 million hospital, which ultimately was not needed.

Any understanding of the whole field of mental health programs must start with an understanding of the distinction between the mentally ill—who are incapacitated for varying periods because of psychotic disorders—and the mentally retarded, who are more or less permanently incapacitated because of inborn or injury-induced physical defects. To many of us, the most tragically moving condition is mental retardation in children, resulting from congenital defects. Through my years as Attorney General, I was frustrated by an inability to respond to the calls and visits of friends and others who asked my help in getting a mentally retarded child into a state institution. There was always a long waiting list for admission.

When I became Governor, I learned that the formal applicants on the waiting list for admission to hospitals for mentally retarded children numbered more than two thousand. With the existing facilities already crowded and with less prospect for "recovery" than the mentally ill had, the mentally retarded child and his family faced years of waiting for help, and there was no assurance that the child would ever be admitted for full-time care and treatment. It would have been fine, economically and politically, if the private sector of society had been able to care for the mentally retarded children of California. But the cruel fact was that these children were not being cared for properly, and families were being destroyed as a result.

The priority and urgency were established. We did the job that had to be done, through government and through a budget. Dr. Blaine went to work, and the waiting list was eliminated. Many of the severely retarded children were placed in state hospitals as full-time patients. Some were placed in day-care centers to free their families at least during the working hours. Some were put in the care of private individuals who were licensed and paid by the state. The whole effort cost the state money, but I had no doubt that the lives of the children and their families fully justified the cost.

From 1959 to 1967 the mental health effort was not strictly a state-level operation. Through a new law, the Short-Doyle Act, the state provided funds to local jurisdictions to boost their services to the mentally ill and the mentally retarded in their communities. The Short-Doyle program permitted counties and cities in California to modernize and expand treatment that often required specialized competence for local problems peculiar to an area.

When he became Governor, Reagan's approach to mental health was noisy, confusing, vacillating, amateurish, and based on the most fallacious and narrowest economic viewpoint. He not only ordered a $17.7 million and 3,700-employee reduction in mental health programs but also called for the closing of fourteen outpatient psychiatric clinics and the elimination of such special facilities as the Mendocino State Hospital's 400-bed Alcoholism Treatment Center. He ordered the "deactivation" of eighty wards in ten state hospitals and approved plans to fire hundreds of psychiatric technicians who were receiving in-hospital training to improve their competence. California's mentally incapacitated, I feared, would rapidly return to the care of the "bughousers."

It was clear that Reagan had not properly studied the state's mental health program needs and had no idea of what he was doing beyond the boastful, arbitrary, and drastic cut in the total program. He insisted that the huge budget cuts and personnel reductions would not lower the quality of patient care—an impossible conclusion even on the basis of common sense.

The new Governor's ignorance of the facts was revealed again and again, as, for example, in his press conference of April 4, 1967:

QUESTIONER: Governor, you said that you hoped the counties would be able to pick up the cuts. The County Supervisors Association has said they wouldn't be able to pick up those cuts. Do you have any comment on that?

REAGAN: "I'll wait to see what the individual county supervisors say.

QUESTIONER: Do the hospitals have discretion under Civil Service? Can they lay off people who are permanent staff?

REAGAN: Well, I'm not going to get into the complicated area of all of those rules, because, very frankly, I only know there are many of them and I'm not familiar enough with them.

It is commendable when a public official occasionally admits he does not have enough information to answer a question, but the pattern was all too regular with Reagan. Here he was, advocating a massive cutback among mental hospital personnel without the slightest idea of the rules by which his mandated cutback would have to be implemented. One could forgive him, perhaps, if one did not realize that he had a huge staff and was, as are all public officials, briefed in advance of sessions such as this one. One can only conclude that Reagan would have accepted the firing of all the state's best-trained personnel in order to achieve his cutback. At any rate he remained ignorant and showed it in his press conference of April 11:

> QUESTIONER: Exactly how will the in-patient treatment of alcoholics be handled to replace the program at Mendocino State Hospital, since there is no other similar treatment available for these patients either on the state or county level?
> REAGAN: Well, I can't answer that for you right now because there are a lot of details in this that we are still studying.

In his press conference of April 25:

> QUESTIONER: Governor, on mental health, have you had a chance to read the Commission report on staff and standards?
> REAGAN: No, this is in the hands of our Department [of Health and Welfare] now, and I haven't.

In his press conference of June 13:

> QUESTIONER: Isn't it true that, for example, at Sonoma [State Hospital] there are fewer staff available to treat the patients than there were in January?
> REAGAN: There may be some fewer. I don't know.

The new Governor and his staff assistants spoke vaguely
of a "two-month study" on which he had based his decision
for the massive cutback in mental health budget and
personnel. When asked by members of the legislature to
produce çopies of the study, Reagan's assistants refused with
the excuse that the study was in the form of "in-house work
sheets." Assemblyman Winfield Shoemaker concluded that
the absence of any report "indicates why the legislature and
the public are suspicious that there may not have been any
study at all." That may seem like a harsh conclusion, but,
despite the fact that the Governor and his program were
coming under heavy and continuing fire, no such data were
ever put into finished form and made public.

Call it uncharitable if you will, but I regretfully conclude
that the Governor thought he could push his cutback
program across with nothing but his considerable personal
charm and salesmanship. This is not an inconsistent view,
given the Governor's own assessment of himself as an
"amateur" and his staff's admission that they were,
collectively, "amateur amateurs." Only an amateur could
make such a critical error in assessing the need for facts to
support such a sweeping "reform" program.

There was other evidence that Reagan had swung his
economy ax on mental health programs without any
understanding of the facts and consequences. Early in the
year he acknowledged that he had not personally visited any
of the state's mental hospitals as Governor. Through the
spring and summer he was repeatedly asked at his press
conferences if he planned to visit any of the hospitals. He
repeatedly answered that he had no such plans. And, at
times, while the whole mental health program was in
confusion and thousands of lives hung in the balance,
Reagan's attitude was downright breezy. This exchange took
place in his press conference of April 25:

QUESTIONER: Governor, you say you are going to Los
    Alamos to see the atomic plant, because you want to

get a firsthand look as a regent [of the University of California]. Yet you don't want to visit, say, a state mental hospital . . . because you don't feel you are qualified in that field. What is the distinction; are you more of a scientist?

REAGAN: Well, I think you are trying to compare apples and oranges. Incidentally, speaking of that, I owe the Governor of Pennsylvania a case of oranges.... I have not been immune to looking at institutions of that kind. I have been in a number of mental hospitals, not since I've been Governor. The thing that we are dealing with is factual information on the part of these institutions. . . .

By this time it was abundantly clear that there was precious little factual information behind the Reagan proposal. Mail appearing in newspapers around the state was overwhelmingly adverse to his plan. If stubbornness is a virtue, Reagan is virtuous indeed. But taste is a virtue beyond argument, and that offhand remark about the crate of oranges, tossed gratuitously into a supposedly responsible answer to a very serious question, raises doubts about Reagan's basic good taste.

Reagan finally concluded late in the year that he should indeed visit a state mental hospital. In late November he toured California's largest mental hospital at Camarillo. But that visit seemed far less a fact-finding mission than a staged response to public indignation over his apparent in-difference to the human conditions in the hospitals.

Immediately after Reagan's tour at Camarillo, the Union of State Employees charged that it was a "peek-a-boo glance" and that a Hollywood-type setting had been arranged in advance for the Governor's announced visit. The union's officials said that, for the day of Reagan's visit, new clothing was issued to patients, additional shifts of employees were put into duty in the wards, and bare spots in the lawns surrounding the hospital had been dyed green.

The charges may have been exaggerated, but Reagan's reaction to them was revealing: "Even in-laws sweep the carpet and polish things up when you come for a visit," he said. "That's a matter of pride in your work. Citizens can come through here at any time. There is no special point to my making such visits."

Reagan missed the whole point that the press had been trying to make: that it is difficult for a Governor to gather facts and learn the truth without firsthand, unannounced looks at a state program. I did this often as Governor. During my terms I visited personally every mental hospital, every prison, and almost every other state facility in California. And the key to the success of those visits was that they were not announced in advance. On these visits I did not want a ballyhooed publicity circus; I wanted to see the mental hospitals operating the way they normally were, without benefit of a "sprucing up" to impress me. Frequently I literally slipped into a mental hospital by the back door, alone or perhaps with only one aide.

When various professional associations and groups of employees in the mental health field began active opposition to Reagan's decisions, he heatedly denounced what he called "blackmailers" and "a high-powered propaganda campaign." At one point he characterized the state's mental hospitals as "hotel operations." A Danish medical official visited a California hospital for the mentally retarded and remarked, "I could not believe my eyes. In our country, we wouldn't treat cattle that way." Reagan reacted by condemning "outsiders" but also ignored suggestions for a study of California hospitals by a team from the Menninger Clinic or even by a group of California experts. When 650 members of the Southern California Psychiatric Society approved a resolution calling the cutbacks "disastrous," Reagan called them "headshrinkers."

In the midst of the controversy over the mental health slashes, Reagan was often imprudently angry and rude in his reaction to criticism. A few times, however, he responded with a jocular quip, which—to me—was shocking, in light of the human tragedy and seriousness of the situation. These comments came in his press conference of June 13:

QUESTIONER: Governor, a spokesman for the Psychiatric Societies of California, Dr. Irving Phillip, says California is not number one regarding the treatment and care of mentally ill.

REAGAN: This is a technicality. . . . I will challenge him, with regard to the mental health care for the patient, that we are considered throughout the nation to be the leading state. . . .

QUESTIONER: He also says you have to be under great strain personally to [charge] blackmail to the entire medical profession.

REAGAN: Well, you know, a headshrinker, he's probably sitting there looking at the pupils in my eyes on television. He can see me on a couch now. Well, I want to tell you, if I get on that couch, it will be to take a nap.

That press conference ended with the transcriber's notation: "(Laughter)." The public discussion of the issue had sunk to a ridiculous level, thanks largely to Reagan's intemperate comments and flippancy in dealing with a critically important subject. As for the laughter, here's what one veteran reporter had to say:

"Some of us laughed, sure. What the hell else can you do when you are confronted by something so gross? It would be unmanly to cry. Personally, I used to sit there and look at the guy and say to myself, 'What the hell did California ever do so bad that this disaster has been visited upon it?' I tell you, it was unreal.

"Here was this guy, the governor, doing a kind of Henny Youngman routine, dodging the heavy questions by snapping off responses as though he was putting down a heckler during his night club act. I had to believe it, because I saw and heard it, but I never wanted to."

Reagan also publicly failed to state the truth on many occasions. In his press conference a week after his first announcement of the cutbacks he was asked about the rate of admissions to state mental hospitals (meaning those who were accepted for treatment), as opposed to the number of patients actually in the hospitals. Reagan stated flatly: "The admission rate has been dropping." That was not true: The admission rate was increasing throughout the state in 1967. At Napa State Hospital the admission rate was higher than at any time in its history. After he ordered the elimination of fourteen state outpatient clinics, Reagan said confidently that the local, county-operated clinics would handle the new load. But in September, to offer just one example, the Los Angeles County Board of Supervisors voted unanimously not to take over "aftercare" treatment of state mental health patients because the state had not come through with an increase of funds to help do the job.

Reagan could play loose with the facts, denounce his critics, make jokes about the mental health situation, and for a time stick rigidly to his "nothing is more important than economy" position. But the depth and breadth of the opposition in the state gradually forced him to modify his arbitrary orders and finally to reverse some of them.

The protests of professionals in the field became more intense and more pointed. Many of the San Francisco area's private psychiatrists, psychologists, and educators, whose own practices were not in jeopardy, banded together against what they called Reagan's "terrific blow" to the State Mental Hygiene Program. Irving Rosenblatt, Jr., Chairman of the San Francisco Mental Health Advisory Board, said that "the sweet moment of victory [over mental illness] has turned to the sour taste of despair as a result of the mutilation of the California Mental Health Program by the state administration." Dr. J. M. Stubblebine, chief of San Francisco's Community Mental Health Services, said bluntly that, unless Reagan implemented the budget cuts more carefully, "some patients will die." Generally, the mental health specialists argued that a good system and program should not be scuttled just because it had been successful; the need remained. The responsible critics acknowledged that some reduction of mental health personnel was possible, because of decreasing numbers of full-time patients, but protested Reagan's intention for mass firings with little planning— and no funds—for local alternatives to patient care.

As Reagan's careless and insensitive decisions became more obviously dangerous, the opposition was joined even by some of his most steadfast allies. Republican as well as Democratic leaders and members of the legislature spoke out forcefully against Reagan's cutbacks. The *Los Angeles Times*, which had supported Reagan and maintained a "conservative" editorial attitude toward government economy, at first (March 16) called his mental health cutbacks "a sensible economy move." By March 30 the *Times* had some second thoughts, saying editorially: "Administration spokesmen may find it difficult to answer the charge of 'false economy' in this strange approach to budget cutting." And by April 11 the *Times* was clearly fearful when it asked for assurances from the Governor "that the drastic cutbacks will not wreak havoc on California's mental health program." After studying the facts, the *Times* also stated in its editorial of April 11:

It is true, as the Governor says, that the population in mental hospitals is declining. But his own budget document shows that the number of persons treated in such institutions during the year is on the increase. Furthermore, there is a waiting list for admission to hospitals for the mentally retarded, which administration sources estimate at 1,500, but which some sources claim is far higher. . . .

Furthermore, if reductions in support personnel are found to be based on use of patient labor, then these cuts, too, should be restored. Patients' work can be therapeutic, but to use it as a budget-cutting device strikes us as repugnant.

Strong language for the gray eminence of California journalism.

For a time, Reagan ignored the mounting opposition and insisted that patient care would not suffer as a result of his cutbacks, but the evidence and public uproar over his slashes, much of it stemming from thorough legislative hearings on the issue, did slowly and painfully move him. In an early phase of the battle he agreed to a sixty-day delay in his plans for mass firings of mental health personnel. Through 1967 he grudgingly reversed himself on some of the cutback orders. In 1968, trying to regain some of the loss of popularity on the issue as indicated by opinion polls, he churned out many proposals that would ostensibly improve care of the mentally ill and the retarded. In October 1969, in a speech at Town Hall West, Reagan revealed the full extent of his miraculous public transformation on the issue. Although he began that address (as reprinted in the *Town Hall Journal*) by repeating that "nothing is more important than economizing in government," he proceeded to boast that he had increased the Department of Mental Hygiene budget from $213 million in 1967 to $275 million in 1968!

It is only moderately comforting to find that overwhelming public pressure can convert a Governor of even Reagan's rigid and simplistic viewpoints. But such "conversions" as, in Reagan's case, on the issue of mental health do not have the same continuing impact on public policy as a deeper, personal commitment by the man himself. And the delay in acknowledging and then correcting a major mistake, again as with Reagan and mental health, means months and years of less help and more suffering for thousands of individual human beings. Furthermore, by the beginning of 1970 Reagan had eliminated more than two thousand employees from California's mental health programs, many individual services had been terminated and there were growing problems in the state's mental institutions.

In the summer of 1969 a fourteen-year-old boy was homosexually attacked while he was a patient at Napa State

Hospital. There was no hospital employee on duty in the children's ward at the time of the attack. Reagan's most forceful reaction to the tragic incident was to condemn the press for reporting it. The news coverage of the attack, he said, was "so reprehensible that anyone who has a part in it should be ashamed of themselves." The *San Francisco Chronicle* commented on the Governor's angry outburst:

> It is, of course, not "reprehensible" to call attention to shocking hospital conditions, nor is it an unfair political attack. The state hospital system, as we have noted earlier, is sick itself, undermanned and with a surviving staff of uncertain morale. It is now a system, in many instances, conducive to neglect, violence, and brutality. The California public has not only the right to know about these conditions, and the incidents they spawn, but should know fully of them.

Fuller knowledge came from a study ordered by the legislature and conducted by the public policy research firm of Arthur Bolton Associates. Their preliminary report, issued in January 1970, declared that the state's mental hospitals were so poor that they could no longer be considered "appropriate places" for the treatment and care of mentally disordered children. It declared that treatment was inadequate, crowding in the wards was acute, and living conditions for the children were starkly depressing.

Such reports are valuable, but, even when professionally conducted and graphically written, they cannot convey significant detail, which can come only from firsthand observation. The Reagan Administration not only denied the basic contentions of the Bolton report, but the Governor continued to refrain from seeking firsthand observations of conditions in California's mental hospitals.

I will never forget one example of Reagan's callous indifference to those conditions, and his reliance on formal reports, which occurred in the midst of the mental health controversy in 1967.

In July of that year the Governor defended a plan at DeWitt State Hospital, near Auburn, to serve patients only two hot meals a day instead of three. Questioned about the step at his press conference, Reagan said: "The program they are going to experiment with at DeWitt is an experiment they have been considering quite some time before any talk of economy moves. It is a system that has been put into effect in a number of hospitals through the country."

Reagan had the audacity to suggest that a cutback in the food budget for DeWitt (and other state mental hospitals) would actually result in better and more meals for patients. He referred to "continental breakfasts" and said that the patients would really get four meals a day under the new plan: Rolls, juice, and coffee for breakfast, a hot meal at 11 A.M. another hot meal at 5 P.M. and a snack of sandwiches and milk at 7:30 P.M.

A more accurate and penetrating look at the food situation in state mental hospitals was taken by attorney Paul Berg, a member of the California Association of Mental Health, and James M. Miller, the President of the Sacramento Association for Retarded Children. Berg surveyed the situation at DeWitt and then said: "No one can tell me that the quality of food will remain the same when you fire 20 per cent of the cooks. And to say the food will be 'improved' borders on the ridiculous.

"The pitifully low [food] budget of 79 cents per day [per patient] has been cut by 5 per cent according to a directive sent from the Department of Mental Hygiene to the hospital superintendents April 25, 1967. If the Governor can manage 'improved' nutrition on 20 per cent less staff and 5 per cent fewer dollars for purchase of food, he should be advising every housewife in California how he does it."

His colleague, James Miller, expanded the report: "It doesn't matter if they divide that amount of food into three meals, four snacks, or a combination. It is still a decreased amount of food.

"One noon meal served to a ward of children aged six to

twelve at a nearby hospital for the retarded consisted of watery navy beans, cole slaw, one thin slice of bologna dry around the edges, one slice of bread, and a cup of milk. Half of them didn't touch it. It was unappetizing, cold, and all run together on one dish. And this was the main, big meal of the day.

"This was one month before the 5 per cent cut in food purchase."

At the time this heartless program was being pushed by Reagan there were approximately 20,000,000 people in California. Reagan's boast was that adoption of his plan would save the state $17.5 million annually. This doesn't come to quite 88 cents per capita per year.

It is inconceivable to me that Californians—or any Americans—would have opted for their 88 cents at the expense of those unfortunate mental patients. Even the passing of eight years has not washed the horror of this scheme from my mind. It was positively medieval in concept, a call for the turning of our collective backs upon the mentally ill—and all in the name of economy.

What could one buy with that 88 cents that could obliterate an overpowering sense of guilt?

8
The War on Welfare

Ronald Reagan was elected to a second term as Governor of California in 1970, but by a considerably smaller margin of victory than in 1966. It was becoming clearer to the Republicans and dissident Democrats who had supported Reagan that he was long on talk, short on accomplishment. His "cut, squeeze, and trim" schemes had resulted in four record budgets in a row and ever increasing taxes. Reagan and his advisers saw that, if he were to have any chance at the White House in future, he needed some major accomplishment to run on. Special Reagan task forces identified possible targets; two of these that bore real promise were tax reform and welfare reform.

Reagan's abortive tax reform measure, Proposition One, was defeated by the voters, dealing his Presidential plans a heavy blow. As for welfare reform, the Nixon administration w s pushing a major change in existing welfare programs, a Family Assistance Plan, which would put a floor under every American family's income. Both Democratic and Republican state legislators were endorsing the administration's plan. If Reagan were to follow suit, any credit

that might result would go to Nixon and, in California, to
the legislature. There was no political advantage for Reagan
in supporting the Nixon plan. Furthermore, it smacked of a
guaranteed income scheme and as such was anathema to
Reagan's far-right constituency. Reagan decided to go it
alone on welfare policy. As usual, his attack on welfare
ignored the real shortcomings and the underlying social
problems to concentrate on welfare cheating, a minor matter
by all reasonable standards but an inflammatory issue for
Reagan to exploit.

Welfare programs make a perfect target. Nobody likes
them, perhaps least of all welfare receipients. Few people
understand public assistance. As costs have risen more and
more Americans forget that the purpose of welfare is to
ensure that no unfortunate American citizen lacks at least
enough income to subsist. Even Reagan inadvertently put
part of the truth ahead of his own personal prejudice in this
description of welfare recipients: "Most of these are people
who, either through lack of basic education or lack of any
kind of motivation, lack of any job skill, or maybe just because they just don't want to work—these are the welfare recipients."

Either because he did not know or thought it was not
worth noting, Reagan did not say that welfare recipients also
include the indigent aged, the blind, the disabled, and minor
children. Reagan correctly perceived that welfare was a hot
issue and saw a chance to accomplish in 1970 what he had
failed to do in his first term. That year saw a dramatic
increase in welfare caseloads in California. Recession was a
factor; unemployment rose from 4.4 per cent in December
1969 to 7.1 per cent a year later. Reagan dwelt on the upward
spiral of caseloads and carefully neglected any mention of
recession or unemployment. He was determined to make the
welfare system itself the sole scapegoat.

In vintage Reagan fashion, the Governor said the federally
imposed system was leading the state into bankruptcy. In the
next breath he argued that total welfare reform could be

accomplished at the state level. Knowledgable legislators shared his view concerning the limitations mandated by the federal requirements, and for that reason they were skeptical, to say the least, of his idea that the state could undertake sweeping reforms on its own. That set the stage for an impasse.

In early 1971 Reagan sent down his welfare proposal to the legislature. It was, in the view of many, an extremely regressive program that would effectively dismantle the welfare apparatus. One look and it was apparent that it would never pass. Reagan sought to tighten eligibility requirements for the totally disabled, to deduct federal food stamp and housing subsidies from state payments for all recipients, to limit the amount of job training to be given to adult recipients, limit work-related expenses that employed recipients could deduct in computing their total income, and a host of other regressive cuts. At the heart of the Reagan program was a sort of jackpot idea—an annual maximum welfare pool to cover all recipients' total payments so that any individual's benefits would be reduced as the total caseload increased, regardless of need.

Assembly Speaker Bob Moretti decided to take the fight to the Governor in an effort to salvage any kind of program aimed at cutting welfare costs and eliminating welfare cheats. Here are Moretti's recollections of what transpired:

"The Governor's package had been put together primarily by Robert Carleson, who had recently moved over from Public Works to Welfare. It was punitive and regressive in an extreme.

"What the Governor had been doing in an effort to whip up public support was zeroing in on a half-dozen or so flagrant cases of welfare cheating . . . and making it appear that this was the rule rather than a very minor exception. They found one guy who made $16,000 the year before and was still getting some welfare money, things like that. But there were 2.2 million people receiving assistance in one form or another, and he seemed determined to punish all of them because of a handful of documented cases of cheating.

The votes just weren't there for his program . . . so I called and asked for a meeting. I asked that we meet alone, no aides or staff present, and he agreed. For openers I told him I didn't like him and knew he didn't like me, but that we still had to work together. I told him if he was serious about welfare reform I would be willing to put together a negotiating group to meet with him and whomever else he wanted to hammer out an agreement, line by line, if necessary. I told him that under his plan a great many deserving people would be hurt—and hurt badly. You have to know the numbers of the welfare situation—85 per cent of the recipients are aged, blind, disabled, or dependent children; another 14.9 per cent are the mothers of those dependent children and about one-tenth of 1 per cent are able-bodied men. I don't think many people would want to harm the elderly, the blind or disabled, or little kids if they knew the facts, so I wanted a compromise.

"Reagan agreed. He wanted that welfare 'scalp' so badly he was willing to make a deal. So we met for seventeen days and nights, and we put together the Welfare Reform Act of 1971.

"Reagan participated, but not all of the time. Carleson was no help, constantly taking extreme right-wing positions, but Ed Meece [Reagan's executive assistant] was very helpful in putting together the final bill. Reagan staged a few temper tantrums, pounding the desk and all that . . . but we responded in kind and he discovered that wasn't getting him anywhere. I served more or less as an arbiter, getting things back on track after a blowup. It was tough, but it worked."

Moretti does not resent the fact that Reagan usurped the credit for welfare reform. "We knew he would run around beating his chest about it, so we decided to let him go without rebuttal," Moretti recalls. Asked if Reagan should be given credit as the catalyst who forced the compromise through his insistence, Moretti said: "Yes, I think that's fair to say. There was a climate of concern in the legislature, but whether we would have done anything on our own is problematical."

Moretti shares the view that welfare and tax reform measures were seen by Reagan as important building blocks for a Presidential campaign. Unlike less charitable critics, Moretti does not ascribe Reagan's motives entirely to politics:

"I think he really believes all of his own attacks on welfare. You must remember he is a guy who sees everything as all good or all bad—no gray scale at all. He really became convinced that a handful of cheats represented all the people on welfare. In addition, he doesn't understand—makes no effort to understand—that 85 per cent of all welfare recipients depend on the program for everything they have and that they could be thrown out on the street to starve without their welfare checks. His answer, and he's sincere when he says it, is that they ought to work if they want to eat."

I asked Moretti if he had ever seen Reagan demonstrate any compassion for the unfortunates on welfare.

"No," he said, "nor for anyone else, either."

The Welfare Reform Act went into effect in October 1971 and undoubtedly brought about reductions in the welfare rolls. The question is, how much did the new law actually accomplish, and how much of the improvement was the result of other related factors?

There are few, if any, people in public life today who do not regard welfare as an unholy mess. Welfare laws and administrative regulations are a maze in which the uninitiated can wander forever. There is a growing burden of opinion that the entire system as it exists should be scrapped and a fresh start made. There is dissatisfaction at every level of government as well as among working Americans whose tax dollars feed the system. I choose to believe, however, that we have not retreated so far from our basic principles that very many of us wish to punish the deserving recipients in the process of reform.

Statistics show that 85 per cent of all welfare recipients are aged, blind, or disabled. These individuals own little or nothing. More than half have no income save their welfare benefits. These aged, blind, and disabled welfare recipients scarcely knew there was a difference after "reform." Many of them received larger benefits due to the legislature's insistence that the act contain a cost-of-living escalator. Even with that escalator benefit, scales were below the national standard of need, which amounted to $314 a month for a family of four. Aged, blind, or disabled couples or single persons received considerably less.

Reagan's principal target groups were families with dependent children. These recipients were the villains of most of his horror stories. They were pictured as dissolute, congenitally unemployed (and most frequently unwed) mothers who kept having children to increase their welfare benefits. Examples can be (and were) found to shore up that simple thesis, but they comprised only a small percentage of all recipients. High birth rates among the impoverished are a social problem of considerable magnitude, but Reagan preferred his simple attack to a discussion of the real problem.

The Welfare Reform Act struck at those receiving Aid to Families with Dependent Children. This breaks down into two subcategories, family groups (AFDC-FG) and un- employed (AFDC-U). Much of the progress Reagan claims in cutting welfare rolls relates to a reduction among AFDC U recipients. There are a few facts that must be examined in relation to Reagan's boasts of success.

To begin with, unemployment in California stood at 8.8 per cent at the beginning of 1971. Before Welfare Reform went into effect, the Nixon administration imposed federal wage-price controls, lent $250 million to the giant and ailing Lockheed Aircraft Corporation, and extended unemployment benefits to a maximum of thirty-nine weeks, all boosts to the economy. Claims among AFDC-U welfare clients had begun to drop before the new act took effect.

In 1971 there were 87,737 new AFDC-U applications, more in the early months and less after the federal government actions. The new application rate fell steadily, as unemployment fell, throughout 1972, and by the end of 1973 it had dropped to 56,341. Unemployment by that time was down to 7.0 per cent. The two statistics correlated closely. Most experts believe the welfare caseload would have fallen without the new law, and some go so far as to say it had no effect whatever in the AFDC-U category, where the principal savings were realized. There was a small drop in AFDC-FG caseloads but this was temporary; while direct correlation cannot be made to employment, it is reasonable to assume that greater availability of jobs was a factor.

Reagan's claim about turning the corner on welfare costs does not look so good when the question of unemployment rates is taken into account. There is an additional and perhaps even more important factor involved in this attempt to assess the success of the Reagan plan: the remarkable slowdown in the growth of California as it relates to in-migration. The accompanying figures from the state Department of Finance illustrates the magnitude of this change.

The drop in 1970 reflects the economic malaise. Job opportunities in California had dried up, and few people made the move west without a job awaiting them. The same was true, of course, in every subsequent year, varying only in degree, but the most significant datum is the sheer numerical loss. California had a one-year eligibility requirement for all but absolute emergency aid, and as the migratory rate slowed the dropoff was reflected in the welfare caseload of the subsequent year.

There were no hard figures available, but an educated guess can be made that California actually lost population during the years in question relating to in-migration versus departure figures. This would leave the birth rate, which also had dropped off, as the only source of population gain. Whether that is fact or not, it is obvious that California was not growing at anything like its historic rate, and that quite naturally meant lower welfare caseloads.

MIGRATION TO CALIFORNIA

	Civilian Population	New Migration
1963	17,198,000	357,000
1964	17,714,000	315,000
1965	18,182,000	263,000
1966	18,499,000	180,000
1967	18,871,000	233,000
1968	19,147,000	128,000
1969	19,458,000	121,000
1970	19,690,000	15,000
1971	19,960,000	44,000
1972	20,218,000	55,000
1973	20,461,000	55,000

There is no question that welfare reform rooted out a few welfare cheats, either because of all the publicity or through implementation of the act itself. But this is a far cry from the sort of accomplishment claimed by Reagan. One more table, compiled from state budget documents relating to payments to children, may serve to make the point.

You will note a total caseload drop of about 25,000 from 1971–72 fiscal year figures to those of 1973–74. Compare this with the population figures in the previous chart, and it becomes apparent that the growth slowdown alone could account for the drop. It is also worth noting that California was able to reduce the pool of indigent unemployed, again due to the lower in-migration figures, and that the total caseload drop is more than accounted for by the drop in

AFDC CASELOAD FIGURES

	Number of recipients			Total cost (in millions)		
	1971–72	1972–73	1973–74	1971–72	1972–73	1973–74
Family groups	1,332,155	1,287,294	1,346,575	$ 974	$ 953	$1,042
Unemployed	216,862	185,918	180,755	159	127	129
Institutions	34,488	31,192	30,800	69	70	74
Totals	1,583,505	1,504,404	1,558,130	$1,202	$1,150	$1,245

AFDC-U cases alone. Total welfare costs actually rose slightly during the three-year period. When one considers that the boom was over in California one can understand that Reagan's assertions are grossly exaggerated. He deserves and generally gets credit for focusing attention on the growing welfare problem, but his claims of reducing welfare costs by more than a billion dollars simply are not true. Interestingly, the claims are not made in such precise terms any more, because statistical data proving them to be false, or at the very least misleading, is readily available.

Other aspects of the Reagan program are scarcely mentioned at all any more. An antifraud program, which used computers to check welfare recipients' incomes and employment records, proved so costly and unproductive that it was quietly abandoned, and no figures are available on its effectiveness while in use. The highly touted Community Work Experience Program, which required all able-bodied welfare recipients to accept at least twenty hours of unpaid work a week to retain their eligibility, was structured for 58,776 participants. In fact, only 1,134 participated in the first year, and only 1,040 in the first nine months of the second year. There just weren't many able-bodied welfare recipients, a fact Reagan has not admitted publicly to this day. One survey, conducted by the legislative staff, disclosed that only 262 participants in the CWEP subsequently found regular jobs, and the bulk of them were farm workers. The 1974 legislature enacted a bill abolishing the program, but

Reagan vetoed it just before leaving office, saying the results indicated the tests should continue. The results certainly did not indicate any such thing, but to sign the bill would have been a tacit admission by the Governor that his claims about able-bodied welfare recipients were a straw man from the start.

Reagan still sees his attacks on welfare as a political plus, and he very likely is right. He is wrong when he characterizes the program as a grab bag or cornucopia for chiselers. Welfare is desperately needed by a host of poor people who, because of age or infirmity and an almost total lack of either assets or income, could not exist without assistance. And as for aid to children, the picture is nowhere near as bleak as Reagan paints it. Statistically, birth rates are down among welfare families, from 3.0 children per family ten years ago to 2.2 children today. However, there is a marked increase in the number of one-parent families, and the single parent with small children is severely handicapped in a quest for work or ability to hold a job if one is found. As Bob Moretti put it:

"A welfare mother with three children received $280 a month at the time of reform. If she found work she also had to find a baby-sitter, no mean feat. Welfare recipients statistically are unskilled, so jobs available to them are low-paying. By the time the working mother pays the costs of transportation, taxes, and other incidentals, then pays the baby-sitter, she has less money left for her children and the necessities of food, shelter, and clothing. She simply can't get by, and it is unrealistic to expect her to try."

I share Moretti's view that welfare reform, to be meaningful, must be accomplished at the federal level. Further, it must be done in a humane fashion, recognizing the very real need of the vast majority of recipients and avoiding the polemics of Reagan's broadside accusations. Among those disenchanted with welfare as it exists today, perhaps standing first among the disenchanted, are the recipients themselves.

It is not right that elderly persons without private means

should be subjected to the humiliation of the present welfare system. The American spirit is demeaned when the aged, the crippled, the blind, and unfortunate children are made scapegoats, kept in abject poverty, and reviled by a resentful and unthinking minority whose resentments are whipped up by unreasoned attacks. It is the system that is at fault, not the recipients.

I find I must make another personal digression at this point. The legislative leadership in California stood with Reagan on the question of reform, but they supported President Nixon's Family Assistance Plan. The Governor, because he could see personal political disadvantages in the Nixon plan, adamantly and vigorously opposed it while insisting that the state could solve the problem. I believe the facts show how wrong he was. In 1968 (and 1969) I served on President Johnson's Commission on Income Maintenance Programs under the able chairmanship of Ben W. Heineman, president of Northwest Industries, Inc. My fellow commissioners represented a cross-section of social, political, and economic forces in the United States. The panel could not be characterized as either liberal or conservative. We adopted a report calling for a supplement to low incomes as a basic tool to eliminate poverty. We called it an Income Maintenance Program. I'll let the chairman speak, quoting part of the final report to the President, who was by then Richard Nixon: "Our basic conclusions are that, even if the existing welfare and related programs are improved, they are incapable of assuring that all Americans receive an adequate income."

I concurred in the report, which called for income maintenance at a minimum level of $2,400 annually, even though I and others felt that this was too modest a goal. Julian Samora, a professor of sociology at Notre Dame University, felt impelled to submit a personal supplement, which I quote here in part:

> Someone once said that the poor you will always have with you. This will be true in our society as long as we

do not make a long-range concerted effort to eliminate poverty. We have the means to eliminate poverty as we have the means to go beyond the moon. The Commission's recommendations are a step toward the elimination of poverty, but they fall far short of the goal.

Many would argue that such a program would be expensive, and they are right. The money is available but being spent on other things: billions of dollars for war and war-related activities, billions for space, billions for foreign aid, and billions for farm subsidies.

If this country would reorder its priorities, perhaps we could take care of the poor first.

Reagan has already made it plain that as President he would take the federal government out of welfare and a host of other social programs and turn them over to the states to implement or not as they saw fit. This was part of his pie-in-the-sky $90 billion tax saving plan. Any saving that would result, of course, could be realized only by abandonment of the programs by individual states. Asked what poor people could do if their state saw fit to leave them without assistance, Reagan said they could "vote with their feet," meaning they could move to another state. This callous and indifferent response ignores two very basic points: First, poor people cannot move with the ease of the rich; second, what would happen to those enlightened states that saw fit to continue to meet public responsibilities toward the unfortunate? One can surmise they would become welfare impacted areas if Reagan's victims found a way to move.

Reagan's "plan," of course, is utter nonsense and totally beyond his capability to enact, two facts he may have to admit sooner or later if he can't shake the $90 billion albatross completely. It is significant only because it affords an unusually sharp look at the radical, superficial, and compassionless man behind that perpetual Mr. Nice Guy facade.

9
No Time for the Disadvantaged

It has been many years since poverty has come close to touching Ronald Reagan. In the early 1950s Reagan was making $3,500 a week as a film actor. He saved his money, invested it wisely in real estate, and today is a very wealthy man.

Neither has Reagan made any discernible effort to learn anything about poverty. There is no record of his visiting Watts or Hunters Point or any of California's ghetto areas during his eight years in Sacramento. He made few appointments of minority members to meaningful positions in his administration, and those few were described by the state's minority leadership as "safe Republican friends of the Governor."

Thus the problems of minorities remain a mystery to him. His friends and closest associates show the same disinclination to get involved with the poor and disadvantaged. These people who exert a profound influence on Reagan pay scant attention to the problems or the desires and aims of minority citizens, and neither does Reagan, if one can judge from his record.

When one examines the ease with which Reagan shed the liberal thinking of his friends and associates of years ago and adopted the cast-in-concrete right-wing ideas of his more recent associates, the only logical conclusion one can draw is that Reagan wants to "belong" to a peer group and is willing to accept their ideas as his own if that is the price of admission. This becomes apparent in reading his own chatty autobiography, *Where's the Rest of Me?*, as well as in even a cursory examination of where he has stood at various times in his life.

The title of the autobiography was taken from a line of dialogue in one of his best films, *King's Row*, spoken when the character he played awakened after surgery to amputate his legs. That was play-acting. Today, the question might better be where Reagan's heart and head are. They are, as always, precisely where his current peers wish them to be.

In his book Reagan spoke with feeling about his youth and remembered that it was sometimes blighted by poverty. His father, John Edward Reagan (who once said his son "looks like a fat Dutchman" and thereby gave him his nickname, Dutch), was a victim of the Depression. Unemployed for many months, the elder Reagan campaigned in Illinois for Franklin Delano Roosevelt in 1932 and later went to work in the National Relief Administration. At one time he was in charge of the local Works Progress Administration office. Reagan himself was once an ardent fan and supporter of FDR and his social programs, but he later abandoned these positions to become a vocal critic. He apparently found it easy to forget that his father's troubles and his family's brief experience with poverty were ended by those programs, which were designed to fill a void left by the private sector.

He was, however, still liberal when he was recruited into the Screen Actors Guild in 1938 by Helen Broderick. Reagan rose rapidly in the organization to become an officer and a director. He was impressed by his peers in Guild management, names like Eddie Cantor, Alan Mowbray, Boris

Karloff, James Gleason, Groucho Marx, George Raft, Jimmy Cagney, Gary Cooper, and Fredric March, to name just a few. Reagan applauded vigorously when Eddie Cantor stood up in a guild meeting to tell members, the press, and the public, "I am in the Guild not for myself but for the little people in this industry." Ninety per cent of the Guild's members, then and now, do not make a living at their art. Cantor's concern for the part-time, low-paid performers was well-founded, and Reagan mirrored his views. This may be the last recorded instance of Reagan's expressing any concern for the poor and unfortunate. It is, at least, the last time he demonstrated his concern by personal action.

His record in dealing with the poor, a euphemism for minorities in California, is abysmal. His lack of concern amounts to outright disdain. Reagan told Mississippi reporters in 1973, "if there is a Southern strategy I am part of it." He has become the GOP darling of Dixie. He raised $130,000 for Mississippi Republicans on that occasion, a $100-a-plate dinner, and was told by Gil Carmichael, who ran for the Senate on the GOP ticket a year earlier: "You're one of the key people we need. We have loved you for a long time."

During his eight years in Sacramento Reagan steadfastly opposed fair housing, aimed at ending segregation of the minorities, calling it "forced housing," a polemic since applied vigorously to school busing, which Reagan also opposes. He supported real estate interests in their efforts to confuse Californians about fair housing. Reagan and other spokesmen drummed away at the absolutely erroneous idea that fair housing laws would *force* a homeowner to sell to a minority buyer even if he could not meet the terms of the offer to sell. This was patently false. California's fair housing laws simply said that a buyer could not be turned down *solely* because of race. The law did not in any way relieve a minority member of the necessity to meet all financial requirements imposed on *any* prospective buyer by the seller.

During his last term as Governor, Reagan adopted the Nixon Administration's cynical attitude of "benign neglect" in relation to minority problems. Reagan has repeatedly stated that he is not a racist, and I believe him. Nevertheless, his simplistic statements concerning racial problems—and his unfortunate proclivity for the offensive one-liner—got him in trouble frequently in his administration's early days. One can assume that he learned from those experiences that he would be better off to say little or nothing and hope racial problems would disappear.

Soon after he became Governor, Reagan angered a group of black legislators who met with him in his office. They reported that he regarded the fair housing law as a form of fascism, and quoted him as saying: "You wouldn't want to sell your house to a red-headed Kiwanian if you didn't want to, would you?"

In his press conference of July 25, 1967, Reagan showed a typical lack of restraint in discussing the volatile situation in black ghettos and also revealed the superficiality of his efforts to learn something from blacks themselves in this exchange with newsmen:

QUESTIONER: You met with several of whom you called "responsible Negro leaders." Later on Senator [Mervin] Dymally [now Lieutenant Governor] and other Negro leaders complained . . . that you really did not meet with the men and women who have a following and an influence on the streets of the Negro communities. What is your reaction? . . .

REAGAN: Well, it depends on the kind of following he is talking about. If he means am I going to have a meeting with Stokely Carmichael, no. . . . Senator Dymally's criticism was unwarranted. . . . We had a good meeting. . . . These were what could be called responsible, leading citizens in their various professions and communities. . . .

QUESTIONER: Assemblyman Willie Brown [a black] added
   a little bit to that charge about the Negroes that you
   met with last week. He said that all but one of them
   were Republicans and that they also had some
   connection with your '66 campaign.

REAGAN: How else could I get acquainted with them? This
   is true. It may come as a shock to Willie Brown to
   discover I am a Republican, but I don't think there
   was anything wrong with being with the leadership
   of my own party—and that's what they were.

The Governor continually insisted that turmoil in black
ghettos was the work of a minuscule percentage of blacks
whom he labeled "mad dogs," and he remained ignorant of
the pattern of discontent and anger spreading through black
communities. He also wrote off the causes of the riots,
alleging that they stemmed from some sort of conspiracy, but
he couldn't back up that view with any facts, as in this
exchange in his July 25 press conference:

QUESTIONER: Do you think these riots are being set up on
   some kind of a nationally organized basis?

REAGAN: I think it would be pretty naïve to think these
   riots are just spontaneous. We have read statements in
   your own papers that authorities have identified in
   each riot . . . the presence of the same individuals who
   seem to be traveling a circuit. I just don't believe these
   are spontaneous uprisings. I think there is a plan. . . .

QUESTIONER: If there is a plan, will you elaborate to some
   extent on who you believe is doing the planning?

REAGAN: What?

QUESTIONER: Will you elaborate on who you think is
   doing the planning, if as you say, there is a plan?

REAGAN: No. You would have me guessing then and you
   would have me trying to name names and establish
   guilt or innocence on the part of individuals, and I am
   not an investigating agency. I don't have access to
   that information.

In California, Reagan occasionally acknowledged "legitimate grievances" among blacks. Outside the state, however, he seemed more ambivalent. He was, to put it most kindly, lukewarm about civil rights legislation. At a Republican fund-raising dinner in Columbia, South Carolina, he said:

> Everybody is entitled to equal rights, and it is the obligation of the federal government to enforce those rights. Maybe, in some cases, though, the problem is solved for some at the expense of taking away the constitutional rights of others.
>
> It doesn't do good to open doors for someone who doesn't have the price to get in. If he has the price, he may not need the laws.
>
> There is no law saying the Negro has to live in Harlem or Watts.

That, of course, is arrant sophistry. What was needed in California was an affirmative piece of legislation to do away with discrimination in housing. The law that had been proposed offered no economic concessions to minority members; it simply prevented discrimination against a qualified buyer solely on the grounds of race. Most fair-minded persons will recognize that the absence of such affirmative legislation amounts to *de facto* segregation on the basis of race, and not on economic grounds as Reagan would have had them believe.

Reagan's repeated criticisms of fair housing laws made it easier for others to articulate their prejudices without admitting bigotry. The rallying cry of the real estate industry became "nobody is going to tell me I *have* to sell my house to a [here fill in the minority designation] if I don't want to." Of course, nobody was trying to tell people that, a fact Reagan and others steadfastly ignored.

His vacillation on the issues of segregation and discrimination was apparent again at the National Governors Conference in Cincinnati, Ohio, in July 1968. At that conference Michigan's George A. Romney introduced a resolution that called for determined efforts "to maintain law and order with justice; eradicate racial discrimination in employment, in labor unions, and management practices, in the purchase, sale, and rentals of real estate, in the education of children, and in social services." Reagan was the only Northern Governor voting against the Romney resolution. When the resolution was approved—with only four other negative votes, all of them cast by Southern Governors— Reagan hustled to change his negative vote to "abstain." He said he objected to a section of the resolution calling for an end to discrimination "by state, local, and private initiative where possible and by Federal action if necessary." He also told reporters later that he had not "thought fast enough" to abstain when the vote was first taken. That, I am convinced, was one of the least impressive displays of political fence-straddling in American history.

Reagan's deeds—and his inaction—speak volumes. On the "root causes" of poverty, unemployment, discrimination, and unequal opportunities, Reagan's efforts throughout his terms as Governor were negligible. He consistently opposed or cut back budgets for low-cost housing programs. He slashed appropriations for job-training programs. He vigorously and constantly axed state funds for education, including the modest sums earmarked by the legislature for schools in ghetto areas. He steadily condemned federal antipoverty programs and even boasted that, as Governor, he had vetoed more federal antipoverty grants to California than any other Governor, including Wallace in Alabama. He closed down a score of service centers in the state, which were providing help to the minority poor in job placement, training, and other opportunities. He mocked the federal "War on Poverty" effort and launched his own "war on welfare" crusade. He fought to scuttle the state's "Medi-Cal" program, of benefit primarily to the elderly and the minorities, and denounced the legislature and the courts when they kept that program intact.

California's problems of poverty and social tensions are

not limited to black citizens, who comprise 8 per cent of the population and reside mainly in the larger cities. The state's Mexican-Americans, comprising 13 per cent of the total population, have suffered acutely from discrimination and poverty. By many measurements of economic and social disadvantage, California's Mexican-Americans are in worse shape that the state's blacks, partly because of the language barrier and particularly because many of them live in rural areas where they work as farm laborers. Hunger, deplorable living conditions, poor health, and inadequate educational opportunities stifle the state's Mexican-Americans as much as, or more than, blacks.

Reagan's approach to the problems of Mexican-Americans was every bit as negligent as his attitude toward blacks. His budget-slashing, war-on-welfare policies slowed progress by both groups. If his governmental policies toward the needs of blacks were reactionary, his official approach to the problems of the Mexican-Americans in rural areas was feudalistic.

He invariably sided with growers and corporate farmers against farm workers in struggles to improve conditions for workers. He shared the callous attitudes of Senator George Murphy toward the "bracero" program—the importation of Mexican nationals at low wages to work in California fields. (Murphy, arguing against an end to the "bracero" program, once said that Mexicans were more suitable for stoop labor in the fields than Americans because "they are built different-ly.") Generally, Reagan has concerned himself more with the threat of violence by Mexican-Americans than with the "root causes" of their discontent: serflike working conditions and impoverished living conditions.

In 1966 farm workers in California rallied around a new leader, Cesar Chavez, and struck the grape growers in Delano, a Central Valley city largely dependent on agriculture for its economic viability. After nearly two years of struggle and bloodshed, Chavez's fledgling United Farm Workers Union won the support of organized labor but the battle was far from over. Chavez sought a state law to ensure his union's right to organize. A friendly word from the Governor, who has repeatedly styled himself a friend of labor, would have helped immeasurably. But at a press conference held on March 19, 1968, here is what Reagan had to say:

> QUESTIONER: Governor, do you support the principle of the Chavez movement, the unionized farm laborers, to give them bargaining power the same as other unions?
>
> REAGAN: I have always said that certainly I can't be an opponent of organized labor, but I've always said that labor should be organized from the ranks of the workers themselves who want this. There is a great deal of evidence to indicate at this moment that he still does not speak for the overwhelming majority of those who are working in that field [many of whom at this time were scabs brought in by growers]. I am opposed to the organizing of labor when it is done from the outside on the basis of a small clique. [Thousands of farm workers were formal members of the UFWA, and all reliable reports confirmed that Chavez's movement had the overwhelming support of the workers.]
>
> QUESTIONER: Aren't your comments tantamount to saying that there shouldn't be unionization in the field? With a fluctuating labor force, how would it be possible for a union to be formed, except by a small group?
>
> REAGAN: . . . Those who believe that you can impose on the farm economy the industrial type of union have failed to see some of the farmers' problems. [Chavez understood that; he successfully fought off an early attempt by the Teamsters Union to organize farm workers although now the Teamsters compete with Chavez's UFWA for contracts.] While I have respected

in the union the right to strike, I don't see how you could possibly have collective bargaining in the farm economy without some protection against calling a strike at harvest time, when there could be no legitimate bargaining and when there could be nothing but coercion and blackmail in such a strike.

Cutting through the evasive language, one can see that Reagan was leaving no option at all to this deprived minority, which was seeking progress. If its members used violent tactics, they were "mad dogs and lawbreakers." If they used peaceful, legal methods at those times of the year they had real bargaining power, they were practicing "blackmail."

Reporters made a final attempt to get Reagan to clarify his attitude toward the nonviolent Chavez:

QUESTIONER: As a labor man, how do you assess Chavez . . . as a farm labor leader?

REAGAN: Well, I've had some difficulty reconciling some of his statements with some of his next echelon and their actions. There has seemed to be a tendency toward disruption certainly on their part in spite of his words. And, again, I say it does not seem to be the grass roots type of organizing that I believe should take place.

As violence continued in California's vital agricultural industry, Reagan changed his tune, but only slightly. During his second term he said in a state of the state speech that there should be a law guaranteeing secret ballot elections for farm workers. As usual, he did not spell out any conditions. Perhaps he was not mindful of the massive problems involved in certifying workers to vote in an election when they are migratory and part of an ever shifting labor force. Reagan, always simplistic, simply suggested elections. In any case, Reagan never sent any farm labor legislation to the legislature, never lent the full weight of his administration to the question, and seemed perfectly happy to end his eight-year tenure with the whole matter unresolved. Then, in a final gesture of good will, Reagan vetoed a bill granting unemployment rights to farm workers.

In conclusion it should be noted that the Governor who succeeded Reagan did, in fact, make labor peace in agriculture a top priority of his administration. In a marathon series of meetings with Chavez, the rival Teamsters, the growers, and other interested groups, the new Governor nailed together coalition support for a farm labor law, the first in the nation, which included not only the secret ballot but a whole series of safeguards against tampering with the right of workers to vote even if they had changed their places of employment. The new law, not quite a year old, may prove to be less than perfect, but it was a major start, and it brought labor peace to California's fields for the first time in many years. (I hope I may be pardoned this prideful aside: The Governor who put his personal prestige on the line to hammer out the law was Edmund G. Brown, Jr., better known to me as Jerry, my son.)

Women fared no better than other "minorities" under Reagan's leadership in Sacramento. Caren Daniels of the Secretary of State's office surveyed the employment picture in 1974 and found some disturbing facts.

No woman was among the fifty-five top officials appointed by the Governor.

Only one woman (Dr. Carolyn Vash) broke into the next hundred top-level positions. Dr. Vash was named chief deputy director of the State Department of Rehabilitation.

No women were in the Governor's cabinet, and only six women held executive positions in the Reagan administration. Of these six, three held jobs legally allocated to women or jobs traditionally accorded to female appointees.

Ned Hutchinson, Reagan's appointments secretary, apparently saw nothing wrong with the situation. "We choose whoever is best qualified for the job," Hutchinson said. "There is absolutely no discrimination in the Reagan administration."

The prestigious California Commission on the Status of Women (created by the legislature during my last year as Governor) had a different view. That body, through Chairperson Anita Miller, retorted that "there is absolutely and unequivocally no doubt that women have been excluded from consideration" when top level positions were filled by Reagan. Miller and executive director Pamela Faust denied that there was any shortage of qualified women, although they admitted that many women did not apply for positions, perhaps partly because of the feeling that they would be written off and partly because they tended to downgrade their own qualifications.

"What does Hutchinson mean by best-qualified?" Miller asked. "If being qualified means having a heavy beard, then obviously no women would be qualified."

Miller and Faust went on to say that the administration appeared to take the position that a woman is incompetent until proved otherwise. They added that "you have to be a sleuth to find out when a good job comes open."

It is difficult to swallow statements about no discrimination when the figures show that in 1974, eight years after Reagan took office and following several years of consciousness-raising campaigns by the women's movement, only two women were employed in the 312 top administrative and directorial positions in his administration.

One of the principal goals of the liberation movement has been the Equal Rights Amendment. Reagan's stand on this question has been characteristically ambivalent; he has switched from a lukewarm position in favor of ERA to one of strong opposition. Maureen, his daughter by his first marriage to actress Jane Wyman, has been critical of her father for this switch. So have many other women. Reagan is fond of saying "I have a scenario for that" when asked a political question—and I have a scenario for his about-face on ERA. It goes like this:

When the ERA passed the California legislature in 1972 it had little effective organized opposition. At that time Richard Nixon was secure in the White House, and it looked to Reagan as though 1976 would be a wide open year in the race for the GOP Presidential nomination. It was politically safe and smart to favor ERA under the existing conditions, provided, of course, one did not go too far. Reagan assumed that stance, somewhat vague but nonetheless, according to daughter Maureen, "seemingly in favor" of the amendment.

Then came the national administration's game of musical chairs brought on by Spiro Agnew's *nolo* plea to felony bribe-taking charges and the slide of Richard Nixon as a result of the countless felonies committed in Watergate and related matters. When Nixon resigned and Gerald Ford became President, it was a whole new ball game for Reagan and other GOP Presidential hopefuls.

President Ford is a very conservative Republican, although he currently does not rate high marks from that wing of his party. With Ford sitting as President, even by appointment and resignation, Reagan could be cut off from his own natural constituency if he wasn't careful. His appeal had always been strongest on the far right, and the female voices of the far right, led by Phyllis Schlafly (Goldwater's number one fan) and the women of Pro America, were sounding off against ERA. These conservative Republican women were of prime importance to Reagan. They were his most enthusiastic audience during four years of stumping America in the conservative (and incidentally his own) cause. They worked in campaigns and they either gave money themselves or influenced their husbands to do so to the candidates of their choosing.

Since Reagan had been less than forthright in his support of ERA, the chameleon-like switch to outright opposition was easy. He began to articulate a series of vague fears about its effect on divorce laws, child support, and rape statutes. He did not forthrightly criticize Ford for his support of ERA but said he was against any law which "encourages sex and sexual differences to be treated as casually as dogs and other beasts treat them.''

This point of view is, of course, almost a verbatim quote from the right-wing women's groups in opposition to ERA. Reagan even shared their trepidations about de-sexed restrooms and the far-out possibility of women's being drafted for combat duty in the services.

Once again, Reagan took on the protective coloration of his peers. The conservative women of America were opposed to ERA for a series of arcane and nearly irrational reasons, but they were, after all, his supporters.

Ronald Reagan, no racist or bigot, a friend of labor and American women, still has an uncanny ability to count votes among his natural constituency and change colors to harmonize with his peers. The political amateur, it seems, can be very professional in a quest for votes.

10
The Inner Circle

Ronald Reagan is a very private man. He made it plain during eight years as Governor of California that he wished to protect that privacy. He avoided social and political entanglements that would pre-empt his evenings or weekends. He delegated much to his staff, but he never befriended most of its members. The relationship was correct and businesslike, with Reagan remaining personally aloof. He was not reluctant to say that he preferred the company of his wife, Nancy, and the security and peace of their own home to the hectic and demanding life-style of more gregarious politicians.

Ironically, the Reagans met because conservative Nancy was upset to discover that another actress of the same name was on the mailing list of the Communist Party newspaper, the *Daily Worker*. She feared that she might be confused with the other woman. This was in 1950, the height of the anti-Communist panic in Hollywood. She was sent to Reagan, then president of the Screen Actors Guild, by movie producer Mervyn Leroy, and that began a two-year romance. They were married in 1952.

Nancy was an actress, as was Jane Wyman, Reagan's first wife, but there the similarity ended. Miss Wyman was a star; Nancy's never shining career was nearing eclipse when she met Reagan. They worked together only once, in his last motion picture, an eminently forgettable low budget film called *Hellcats of the Navy*. Soon after they married, the Hollywood slump was nearing its low point, and Reagan began to experience long layoffs. At first he accepted cut-rate jobs from producers whom he would not even have talked to a few years earlier. Later he became convinced that this course could only destroy his chances to resurrect his career. He tried a nightclub act in Las Vegas, and it was a moderate success, but both he and Nancy were uncomfortable in that environment. "We're not nightclub people," Nancy reportedly said.

In 1954 Reagan was offered by his agents to the General Electric Company as spokesman for the firm with its employees and dealer organizations. He signed for $125,000 a year, but later this was raised to $150,000. Reagan proved to be a super salesman. In the years that followed he met audiences face to face for the first time in his life, save for the interval at Las Vegas. He loved it. But GE was not unreservedly happy. Reagan frequently had trouble fielding questions from workers, dealers, or plant executives, primarily because he had not at that point in his career developed a real philosophy, either of life or of politics.

Ralph Cordiner was president of GE at the time, and he recalled telling Reagan, "Get yourself a philosophy you can stand for and the country can stand for." Cordiner said he believed the real change in Reagan began then. In any case, Reagan began to emerge as a conservative, veering farther and farther to the right as he got more deeply involved with the new peer group of business and industrial leaders. Reagan has always maintained that GE made no effort to censor his remarks, but it should be noted that he struck derogatory references to the Tennessee Valley Authority when it was learned that GE was selling millions of dollars worth of equipment to TVA. Perhaps that was coincidence, but Reagan substituted an attack on another aspect of his developing enemy, big government, one that did no business with GE.

This willingness to bend to outside influences could not be faulted seriously had Reagan remained a private citizen. It is natural for an individual to make reasonable efforts to preserve his own security. Some will go to far greater lengths than others. During these formative years, when he was turning to a career in politics, Reagan attacked every social program from farm price supports to Medicare. He condemned Social Security, asking that it be made voluntary "so that those who can take better care of themselves be permitted to do so," an idea he cherishes to this day.

In 1962 Reagan's "G.E. Theater" suffered a serious setback in the TV ratings, and Reagan's eight-year association with GE ended. By then he was a wealthy man, with large real estate holdings in the Santa Monica Mountains, which he subsequently sold for a very substantial profit. His brother, Neil, an ad agency vice president, sold Reagan to the Borax Company as host for its new "Death Valley Days" series. Once again the big money rolled in. That was in 1964, the year Reagan belatedly got around to changing his registration from Democrat to Republican. He had supported every GOP Presidential candidate since Dwight D. Eisenhower in 1952.

In the year of the Goldwater debacle Reagan was named state co-chairman of Goldwater's campaign. He took the defeat hard, especially the defection of moderate Republicans, who sat on their wallets and their hands as Goldwater was crushed. Reagan denounced them as traitors and warned that conservative philosophies had not been defeated. "No more Republicans with the same socialist ideas as the opposition" was the way he put it in sketching his idea of the GOP's future.

It was at about this time that the late California Secretary of State Frank Jordan sent up his "Reagan for Governor" trial balloon. There was no doubt that Reagan had emerged from the ashes of the Goldwater disaster as a sort of conservative phoenix. He had electrified Republican audiences with "The Speech" and charmed them with his charismatic appearance and style. Reagan had turned on the conservatives as Goldwater had never been able to do.

Philosophically the two were not far apart. Both were hawks on Vietnam. Reagan once advocated "a declaration of war on North Vietnam. We could invade the place, pave it over, and be home for lunch." They stood on the same ground on welfare, Social Security, Medicare, on all the major conservative questions. But where Goldwater was uninspiring as a speaker, Reagan was electrifying. This ability to work an audience into high enthusiasm was Reagan's principal asset, and it is the quality that makes him most dangerous.

Goldwaterism was rejected overwhelmingly, both in California and nationally, but Reagan came out of the campaign with his reputation greatly enhanced. Then, as now, his pronouncements on matters of public policy, both state and national, were oversimplified promises of a brighter new world for the well-to-do, the achievers, and especially the America Firsters. He inherited and perhaps even enlarged the Goldwater constituency and for the first time began to think seriously of himself as a political leader.

There was a curiously coincidental event in that turbulent year of 1964 that certainly encouraged Reagan's new image of himself and did little to discourage his supporters. It could have been considered proof of his assertions that conservative dogma had not been rejected by the voters.

Reagan's old actor friend from SAG days, George Murphy, swam upstream against the Democratic current that year and was elected to the United States Senate over Pierre Salinger. (I had appointed Salinger when Senator Claire Engel died in office, close to the end of his term.) Murphy traded on his movie reputation (he was fond of reminding audiences that he had "always been nice to

Shirley Temple") and was the beneficiary of a perplexingly inept campaign by Salinger, who had a 22-point lead in the first voter poll taken after the primary. Murphy's election was not lost on Reagan. California voters would take an actor seriously, and a stanch conservative to boot.

Nor was it lost on influential Goldwater supporters, still smarting over the extent of their defeat. Among them were Henry Salvatori, an oil developer; Holmes Tuttle, a wealthy auto dealer; the late A. C. (Cy) Ruble, president to Union Oil Company at the time; Los Angeles businessman Ralph Townsend; and a right-wing ideologue, the Reverend W. S. McBirnie, a radio pastor. McBirnie earlier had been associated with Richard Nixon and was largely responsible for some of Nixon's speeches. This group, plus others less prominent but no less conservative, were the prime movers in Reagan's first campaign. Most are still active. Only Salvatori has gone over to President Ford, a conservative himself. Once again, Reagan gave every appearance of responding with knee-jerk simplicity to this heady new peer group. They were the kind of men he had come to admire above all others, big men in industry, movers and shakers. Heady stuff for the one time King of the B Pictures.

The ongoing influence of these men on Reagan was apparent during his two terms as Governor. All were implacable foes of welfare. Many, led by the Reverend McBirnie, were fearful of mental health programs. All loathed taxes. None had any personal contact with California's minorities and frankly didn't give a damn about their problems. There was not an environmentalist among them. Reagan, in his eight years in Sacramento, amply justified their faith in him. He articulated their straight "party line" on all issues.

There were others who found Reagan did not forget his peers and his pals once he got into the governor's office. Take the famous battle of the redwoods ("You've seen one tree," etc.) as a case in point. In the long and controversial effort to establish a Redwoods National Park in California,

Reagan pretended to be a strong supporter of a big national preserve of the magnificent trees along California's North Coast area. In fact, his antifederal attitudes and commercial orientation delayed and often confused the struggle to establish the park.

"I believe our country can and should have a Redwood National Park in California," he said to a U.S. Senate Interior Subcommittee hearing in 1967. But the next day, in Sacramento, he said: "There can be no proof given that a national park is necessary to preserve the redwoods. The State of California has already maintained a great conservation program."

The Governor was slow to support a compromise, sponsored by Senator Thomas H. Kuchel, between the demands of the conservationist Sierra Club and the meager offerings of the lumber industry on the total amount of acreage to be set aside for the park. He bluntly told a congressional committee that he was determined to drive a hard bargain in exchange for allowing two state park areas to be consolidated in the National Park—demanding turnover of certain other federally owned lands to the state. He seemed to ignore the fact that the federal government was willing to invest tens of millions of dollars in a park of benefit to Californians as well as visitors to the state. After Reagan's demands were expressed, the chairman of the House Interior Subcommittee hearing the issue noted, "California should be less demanding. It certainly would speed up things and get us closer to a favorable solution."

In his press conference of July 11, 1967, Reagan also acknowledged that one big barrier to the establishment of the Redwoods National Park was his insistence on additional "protection" for private timber interests. On that date Reagan was asked directly whether or not officials of the lumber company involved, Rellim-Miller, had contributed to his election campaign. Reagan said he didn't know. But his executive secretary later confirmed that Darrell Schroeder, general manager of the firm, had been Reagan's campaign finance chairman in a northern county the previous year.

There can be no question that there was a clear conflict of interest involved. My point, however, is that Reagan had been so thoroughly conditioned by friends like Schroeder to the lumber industry viewpoint that he was an intellectual captive on the question of logging versus parklands.

Reagan's closest advisers were important figures in industry, many with large holdings and substantial interests in California's natural resources. His election was a blow to conservationists and ecologists, and his record over eight years justified the early fears. It was typical of Reagan, however, that he used his now familiar trick to put a different face on the matter.

In January 1970 Reagan devoted one-third of the time and content of his state-of-the-state legislative address to the subject of conservation and environment control; his budget message later the same month called for spending exactly one dollar out of each $516 of state funds for conservation and environment control.

On the vital and then stylish issue of environment control and ecology, Reagan is appropriately eloquent on the subject of pollution, resources control, and the preservation of the world's natural values and beauty. But, as usual, his economy ax cleanly cuts through the promises. One state-of-the-state message by the Governor issued this appropriate challenge: "A booming economy and the 'good life' will be no good at all if our air is too dirty to breathe, our water too polluted to use, our surroundings too noisy, and our land too cluttered and littered to allow us to live decently." Despite that grand-sounding commitment, Reagan took few of the vital steps toward the salvation of California's magnificent natural resources and beauties. He does deserve credit for his water quality control efforts, but that's about all. Otherwise, Reagan equivocated on the pressing problems of environment control. He said that he was for a ban on new drilling for oil in offshore areas of California under the jurisdiction of the state. But he said nothing about halting the continuing drilling of several rigs that were, at that moment, leaking oil into the ocean and onto the beaches of Santa Barbara. And, for the previous year and a half, during which the offshore oil drilling was fouling the beaches and killing wildlife, Reagan had been characteristically evasive. Reagan subtly acknowledged his sympathies for the corporate interest above the broader public interest on the environment issue.

"Progress and preservation are compatible," he said in a well-cadenced and alliterative phrase. "It is the refusal to work together for the proper balance that is incompatible with the spirit of the 'seventies." What that means is that he doesn't think the state government ought to interfere with corporations that, while making their products and profits, foul the water, air, and land.

In 1973, when the energy crisis hit, Reagan seized the opportunity to endorse resumption of offshore oil drilling, the commercial development of the Elk Hills Naval Oil Reserve (a standby pool of oil for possible defense needs) at Taft, California, and a full-speed-ahead program for the development of nuclear energy plants, a controversial hot potato in California. All of these Reagan proposals, one can assume, were greeted gleefully by backers with interests in the energy field.

Reagan continues to this day to boast that California has the "toughest antismog law" in the country. He fails to note that the law exists only because of the dedication of hard-working legislators from both parties and that he never lifted a finger to help assure its passage. On smog, *San Francisco Chronicle* columnist Charles McCabe put down Reagan's conservationist pretensions with these biting comments:

It is the mark of the successful politician that he faces the inevitable, and then takes credit for it.

Jumping on the bandwagon can be made to look like leadership if the move is made dexterously enough.

Which is precisely what our dexterous Governor in Sacramento is presently trying to do with smog, which he has discovered is a hot political issue.

It is a hot political issue because, among other reasons, physicians in one recent year advised 15,000 of their patients to move [because of] emphysema, chronic bronchitis, and asthma.

Governor Reagan . . . recently unleashed a six-point program against smog. Its major provision would convert many of the state government's 25,000 motor vehicles to dual low-emission natural gas and gasoline fuel systems.

As might be expected, the Governor came around too late and with far too little.

Furthermore, he tried to kidnap the smog issue from the man who has really been doing something about it in this state—a Democratic Senator from Oakland named Nicholas C. Petris.

By 1973 it had become clear that the Reagan administration purposely had created a toothless tiger in the California Air Resources Board and that no really tough stances were going to be taken to curb vehicular air pollution. There was no effort made to draw a state plan to carry out the mandates of the 1970 federal Clean Air Act, although the absence of such a plan necessitated a takeover by Reagan's archenemy, the federal bureaucracy, in this case the Environmental Protection Agency. Not only was there no plan, there was consistent opposition to any broadening of either research activities or a regulatory program. Reagan vacillated on a program to control nitrogen oxide emissions from motor vehicles, seemingly fearful of auto industry warnings that such controls could cause engine damage.

Former Republican Assemblyman and later Senator Craig Biddle, an author of much smog legislation, carried the nitrogen oxide control measure. Biddle said his efforts were frustrated and discouraged by the lack of support at the administrative level. "I have to run for re-election and keep telling the voters smog would be a lot worse if it weren't for me," Biddle lamented.

Petris also was a critic of the California Air Resources Board because it fought many of the bills he introduced. Petris said, "The ARB has the duty to solve this problem, or at least provide the leadership. But they're in an intellectual box with the auto industry. They think they have the exclusive wisdom, and anything outside their perception is no good."

The ARB clearly was a captive of conservative politics. ARB member Gladys Meade was one of those summarily replaced by Reagan when the board insisted on a program for the mandatory inspection of automobiles to help eliminate pollutants from exhausts. She blamed an administration rule that there had to be unanimous agreement on all policy questions to avoid public squabbles. Strangely, the Reagan-appointed board finally approved a program calling for mandatory engine tune-ups but turned down the inspection requirements. "How can anything be mandatory without inspection? There can be no enforcement," Meade said. As she left the board, the disillusioned Mrs. Meade said the ARB lacked authority it needed, "but we could at least have tried to meet the practical effect of the federal law, the spirit if not the letter. It isn't our failure alone. It's the failure of the entire [Reagan] administration."

Reagan did not appear to regard it as failure. He was willing to take the advice of the industry, which wanted to avoid any additional regulation, over that of the experts. This is consistent with his belief that business should be untrammeled, and it certainly did not run counter to the wishes of his closest advisers and strongest backers. Then Reagan administered the *coup de grâce*, cutting the ARB budget request from $3 million for research to $1.5 million. Because of the unanimity rule the ARB was in the incongruous position of having to support Reagan and ask the legislature to ignore its own budget request.

(It is worth noting that the new administration in

Sacramento moved quickly to provide new powers to the Air Resources Board. These have been used to levy heavy fines against both Chrysler and American Motors for failing to meet air pollution standards on new cars sold in California. There is a new climate emerging, and clean air advocates have taken heart.)

None of this is to suggest that Reagan is indentured to his political backers. Rather, he reflects their views so precisely as to be an ideal candidate for them. Like any actor, Reagan is used to working from a script. He is a "quick study," as they say in the acting business (witness the mini-memo fixation), and he made a very handsome living for years playing roles that required only that he memorize his lines, not plumb beneath them for hidden meanings, subtleties, or nuances. Long before the computer took over our everyday affairs, Reagan was being "programmed" by writers and directors, molded by producers and studio executives, packaged and sold by promotion and publicity men. He hints in his book *Where's the Rest of Me?*, that this was a somewhat unrewarding experience. Reagan, in short, was the creature of his industry's management and creative organizations. Small wonder he still finds it easy to absorb and adopt the thinking of the people around him. And he is most comfortable with the wealthy, the successful, and the self-assured—a mirror image of Reagan as he sees himself.

This tendency to weathervane or change color to match his environment was noticeable much earlier in his life. There were the boyhood experiences that first made him a Democrat and a stanch supporter of FDR, and for a brief time made a radical student leader out of this otherwise conformist youth. True, he has since repudiated these early leanings, making FDR and rebellious students prime targets in his campaign, but the changes came as Reagan made progress, found new peer groups, and adopted their thinking.

Curiously, he is to this day an admirer of FDR for at least one thing: Roosevelt's ability to "take his case to the people." Reagan told Mike Wallace on a recent "60 Minutes" telecast that FDR had "put the heat on Congress by going over their heads to the people" through his fireside chats on radio. It is a canny perception, and Reagan adopted the same tactic for a while as Governor of California, with mixed success.

His most notable success was with a series of two-minute and fifteen-minute taped reports to the people in his effort to smear all welfare recipients as cheats. His most notable failure was the effort to sell Proposition One, his so-called tax reform initiative with its built-in attempt to undermine if not destroy majority rule in California. But Reagan remains dedicated to the concept of talking directly to the people and will probably do so extensively during his Presidential campaign.

Richard Nixon, who was paranoid about the press, tried taking his message direct to the people over a period of years, beginning with the famous Checkers speech when Eisenhower was about to dump him as his Vice Presidential candidate in 1952. Nixon went farther than Reagan in avoiding open press conferences, especially when the controversy over Watergate and the coverup was at its height. But Nixon met with indifferent success in his direct communications attempts, especially during this period when the evidence against him was piling up. Even when he is rattled, Reagan shows poise on camera, calling on his actor's skills to get him over the rough places. Nixon tried, but this ability always eluded him in large part.

The technique is a good one if the individual involved wishes to make generalized statements that ignore or distort and avoid any rebuttal. It is also useful in selling an idea without the sharp questioning of the press. The Reverend McBirnie, who uses his radio pulpit to fulminate against Communism, among other things, has prospered through the use of such unrebutted speeches, which circumvent knowledgeable examination.

As I write this, Reagan has already run into heavy flak over his proposal to chop $90 billion from the federal budget. On his first day of campaigning in New Hampshire, Reagan took pains to tell the voters there that his plan, which in his own vague generalities would turn a large number of federal programs over to the several states, was no cause for alarm. "I have no intention of imposing either a sales tax or a state income tax on the voters of New Hampshire," Reagan said in his prepared address. Unless I misassess those canny, dollar-conscious New Hampshire voters, they will want a good deal of specific information about the Reagan plan before they buy it. Even William Loeb, archconservative publisher of the *Manchester Union*, has indicated that Reagan's plan would simply shift tax burdens at best. I say it cannot be done unless, of course, the candidate can duplicate (with tax dollars) the miracle of the loaves and fishes.

Reagan came to Hollywood in the 1930s and embraced the Screen Actors Guild with fervor. By his own admission he was greatly impressed by his sudden close association with some of the great names in the glamorous motion picture industry. Then came World War II. Reagan served in a motion picture unit. He could not be said to have returned after the war, because he never really left Hollywood and its sound stages. But he served in his fashion, as he was required, and picked up his Guild activities shortly after being discharged. There was considerable labor trouble in Hollywood over the next several years, largely revolving around jurisdictional disputes between rival craft unions, with the Screen Actors Guild frequently in the middle. There was violence between the Independent Association of Theatrical and Stage Employees (IATSE), led by two thugs named Willie Bioff and George Brown, and the Conference of Studio Unions, under the leadership of Herbert Sorrell of the Painters Union.

Reagan and the Guild vacillated, supporting strikes and crossing picket lines at various times. He loved the real-life intrigues, and once, when threatened with violence, he packed a gun for a period of time. All the while Reagan was busily joining a wide range of organizations, including the United World Federalists, the American Veterans Committee, and the Hollywood Independent Committee of the Arts, Sciences, and Professions. At the time he professed liberalism, and he obviously was under the influence of his peers in the Guild and the various other organizations.

But both the House Un-American Activities Committee and the California legislature's Joint Fact-Finding Committee on Un-American Activities were training their big guns on the film industry. Studio heads, with huge investments in star properties, began to get nervous. So did artist management firms whose livelihood depended on commissions from the earnings of the same artists. Reagan began to pull away from these groups in 1947, a year that saw the California Committee brand Herbert Sorrell "a secret member of the Communist Party," a charge which Sorrell denied immediately. Sorrell later testified before the U.S. House Labor Subcommittee and said, "I am not now nor have I ever been a member of the Communist Party."

These were parlous times, remember, and by the time the same California fact-finding committee branded the Independent Committee on the Arts, Sciences, and Professions "one of the two key Communist fronts in California" Reagan had withdrawn from it and all of the other organizations except for the Guild. There was never any question concerning Reagan's politics or loyalty, but he reacted as did many others at that time and dissociated himself from any group that was even mildly suspect. This comes under the heading of career insurance. The blacklist came into being, and anyone suspected of Communist leanings was in trouble, out of work, and unemployable. Reagan did not want to be counted among their number. Some feel he overreacted to the threat to his career, particularly when he testified before the House Un-American Activities Committee as a friendly witness and admitted: "I do not believe the Communists have at any time been able to use the motion picture screen as a sounding board for their philosophy or ideology."

So much for the Communist takeover of the film industry, at least in the words of Ronald Reagan. Another witness of the period, the late Bart Lytton, a screenwriter who admitted to being a Communist Party member at one time, told the same subcommittee he could recall only one instance when Communist propaganda crept into a production. That was in a WPA theater project years earlier, and it consisted of a derogatory reference to FDR for his failure to leap into World War II immediately after the Soviet Union was attacked by Hitler. The conspiracy, it seems, either was considerably smaller than advertised or considerably less effective.

In any event, Reagan was industriously disavowing his Democratic heritage, although he campaigned later for Helen Gahagan Douglas against Richard Nixon, one of the stars of the HUAC hearings. Two years later he endorsed and worked for General Eisenhower. Although he remained active in the Screen Actors Guild, he was disparaging of AFL-CIO leadership. He did not become an industry anti-Communist activist like Adolphe Menjou, but he stayed clear of any entanglement with the liberal element in the industry. Reagan had heard the voices of his peers—the studio bosses and men like Taft Schreiber at the giant MCA agency—and heeded their words.

The Reagan peer group has always been relatively small. He has not carried many friends from one walk of life to another. No actors are at present listed in the Reagan inner circle, although he had active campaign support from a great many of the better-known conservatives in the industry, such as William Holden, John Wayne, and the late Walter Brennan.

There is agreement among those who know the Reagans well that Nancy, Ronald's wife of nearly twenty years, has exerted a profound influence on Reagan's political thinking. Nancy is the daughter of a wealthy and conservative Chicago surgeon, Dr. Loyal Davis, and she shares her father's political views. Reagan makes it plain that he shares Nancy's devotion to her parents, and it is generally believed among friends that Reagan develops many of his conservative ideas and programs in consultation with his father-in-law. Others say flatly that Reagan's ideas originate with Dr. Davis. In either case, the Reagans visit the Davises frequently, and there is no doubt that Reagan's move to the far right began after he met and married Nancy.

Nancy stands at the center of everything. She and Ronnie are a team, as they both put it. On "60 Minutes" recently, Nancy told Mike Wallace, "Ronnie is my life, my life began when we met." He has made it clear repeatedly that he would prefer to spend his time at home with Nancy rather than anywhere else with anyone else.

Nancy's political views are identical to Ronnie's. Shortly after he announced his candidacy, Nancy told an audience of GOP women that she disagreees with Betty Ford on all of her statements about permissiveness in today's families. She opposes premarital sex, abortion, pot smoking, and the ERA. She is for the death penalty, as is her husband. There is no question among those who know the Reagans best that she has exerted a profound influence on his political career and his political thoughts.

Others in today's inner circle follow the peer group pattern closely. They include Justin Dart, president of Dart Industries; Alfred Bloomingdale, president of the Diners Club; Earle M. Jorgensen, president of Jorgensen Steel Company; and, perhaps closest of all, William Wilson, a publicity-shy and very wealthy southern California rancher and land developer. Reagan's personal attorney, William French Smith, closes the circle. There are other friends, but they cannot be considered close or influential. None of Reagan's staff enjoys this kind of relationship, the closest being Franklyn (Lynn) Nofziger, a former San Diego newspaperman who worked in the Nixon administration,

then became the director of communications for Reagan,
and now heads his Western campaign organization.
Nofziger is the only member of the inner group who is not
independently wealthy, although he has prospered from,
among other things, land speculation in northern California (along with former staff chief Phil Battaglia) while in
Sacramento with Reagan.

There is not a black, a Chicano, a Jew, a poor man, or even
a middle-class working American who has Reagan's ear on
any question. Reagan's input from his closest friends,
people he relaxes with, all comes from the same direction, far
to the right of the mainstream of American political
thought. It is potentially dangerous for a political leader to
isolate himself in such a manner. He seeks to represent the
aspirations, desires, hopes, and dreams of all citizens. He
holds their economic future in his hands, even their lives if
he is President and controls foreign policy. Yet he never talks
directly to any of them. How can he expect to know what
they want, how they feel?

This inner circle is representative of the Reagan constituency in its entirety; narrow but rock-solid, it cannot
tolerate any opposing views. This is the hallmark of the
political extremist, right wing or left. A candidate with less
personal magnetism, less charisma if you will, less ability as
a communicator than Reagan, who harbored such insular
notions would scarcely be a threat, even in today's troubled
America. But Reagan is no Goldwater in that regard, make
no mistake about it. He still is a performer of talent.

One final word from a wealthy auto dealer, Holmes
Tuttle, hammers home the point that the inner circle is most
influential. Tuttle told the *Los Angeles Times* last year that
he regarded Reagan as "a great governor . . . a man of
determination . . . a man who makes decisions regardless of
the political consequences." Then the auto baron added this
telling sentence: "I'd say 80 per cent of my time since 1965
has been spent assisting this administration in the field of
politics."

Or take this quote from Verne Orr, who was Reagan's director of finance, in the same *Times* article on the Reagan years: "It is natural that the type of special interest group that puts you there [in office] is the one that you're going to listen to more closely. In our case it was the conservative groups, the business groups, that put this administration in. They are our constituency."

There is a common belief that a Governor, upon taking office, becomes the Governor of all the people, regardless of politics. Apparently Orr and Reagan do not subscribe to that.

11
Does Reagan Add Up?

In retrospect this book seems more objective than I had dreamed possible at the outset. It deals with the promises, the record of accomplishment, and the ongoing claims of Ronald Reagan and is based on reliable public information that can easily be verified. If it is not a flattering book, the fault lies with Reagan's record.

In calling Reagan a political chameleon I am being descriptive, not derogatory. The chameleon assumes the coloration of his surroundings as a means of self-protection. It is my judgment that Reagan masks his lack of scholarship and lack of an intellectually developed political philosophy by assuming the ideas of others whom he admires, much as the chameleon changes his pigmentation. In both cases it seems to be an involuntary action.

The tiny reptilian chameleon poses no threat. A political chameleon is dangerous, especially if he possesses Reagan's undeniable charisma and ability to communicate. America is still traumatized by the Vietnam War, Watergate, the disgrace and resignation of Richard Nixon, and the floundering economy. Demagogic oratory, full of pie-in-the-sky promises, may fall on responsive ears in these times when doubt, distrust, and personal problems are plaguing so many Americans. In more settled times Reagan could be dismissed as the George Wallace of the GOP. Given the problems of today, Reagan is a force to be reckoned with— and feared.

There are interesting similarities between Reagan and Richard Nixon. I am uniquely qualified to make this judgment, having won re-election as Governor of California by defeating Nixon in 1962 and then lost to Reagan in 1966. I have observed both men from a special vantage point.

Both are very private men with small inner circles of friends limited to a single class and a narrow, unbending political philosophy. As executives, both leaned on a "team" system, preferring to digest staff analyses rather than examine problems firsthand. Both favored minimum government restriction of private enterprise. Both are actively antagonistic toward welfare, and neither ever used the power of high office to assist minorities in their struggle for equality. Both placed government economy above programs to assist the poor. Both had an abiding distrust of the courts, especially in matters involving civil liberties or individual rights.

Despite this litany of similarities, even more important, in my opinion, are the striking differences between these men.

Nixon was a *true* conservative, and he was also a man who demonstrated superior knowledge of the workings of government and a respect for its institutions through most of his career. Nixon was a thoughtful loner, given to scribbling his ideas on a lawyer's yellow pad and deliberating at length over most decisions.

Reagan is a radical conservative. He has a deep and profound hatred of government, especially at the federal level. And he is an impulsive, shoot-from-the-hip battler whenever he slips out of his role as a good guy standing above the battle. Sharp questioning rattles him, and he falls back on the one-liner as a defense—hoping for a laugh to hide the barren responses.

This distaste for searching examination of his radical ideas is becoming more apparent as the national press bores in on his simplistic "plan" to save $90 billion in federal taxes. Reagan proposes to wipe out a host of long-established social, educational, and conservation programs and dump them on the states. He first unveiled this "plan" before a dinner of fat-cat Chicago executives in September 1975. It did not draw heavy fire until he began campaigning three months later. Rather than submit to questioning, Reagan lamely went on the attack, asking: "How come nobody showed any interest in this until now?" George McGovern could have made his ill-fated "$1,000 for everybody" plan public as a senator or a private citizen without causing a ripple, but, as Reagan is learning, a Presidential candidate is held much more closely accountable for the ideas he sponsors. In 1972 George McGovern never managed to shed the albatross of his "plan," as Reagan must know.

When New Hampshire voters questioned Reagan concerning how he proposed to finance all of the federal programs he planned to hand over to the states, he cavilled, assuring them that he had no intention of imposing either a state income or sales tax on them, but failing to respond to the question. And when Ford campaign officials asked the same sort of questions, Reagan again had only a lame rejoinder rather than an answer. Charging that "those people in Washington" were distorting his ideas, Reagan said: "I would like to hear what their proposal is for reducing the size and cost of the federal government."

He fell uncharacteristically silent a few days later when the Ford administration unveiled a new $28 billion tax cut and a same-size reduction in the federal budget.

Most important to any realistic analysis of the Reagan character is the fact that he never suggested once during all of this that his plan was nothing but a catchall collection of ultra-conservative dreams, which had absolutely no chance of being enacted by Congress. Nor did he ever admit that he could not implement such a program without congressional cooperation. I submit that such evasiveness amounts to a conscious effort to mislead voters.

Reagan's debut as a foreign affairs expert was hardly less disastrous. He proposed going "eyeball to eyeball" with the Russians over their involvement in Angola, a dubious *causus belli* if one remembers the lessons of Vietnam. When a reporter in High Point, North Carolina, asked him if his background did not suggest a lack of experience in foreign affairs, Reagan reverted to type: "I know that a large part of dealing in foreign affairs is just the same type of common sense that I found was necessary when, as the president of my union, I sat across the table and had to bargain with management and not blow my cool or give in too soon."

I do not share Reagan's naïve view that bargaining for wages and working conditions for the Screen Actors Guild is an ideal training ground for the Chief Executive of the United States in the minefields of international relations. A more appropriate, direct, and forthright response to the reporter's question might have included an admission that he knew nothing whatever about foreign policy or the intricacies of international diplomacy. Earlier he had confessed to reporters that he could not answer questions about matters in Angola "because I haven't read the newspapers today." It later turned out that he hadn't read them the day before, either.

Reagan came perilously close to breaking his beloved "Eleventh Commandment," "Thou shall not speak ill of another Republican," at least twice on his first campaign swing. His angry accusation that "those people in Washington" were distorting his tax-saving plan stopped just short of attacking the incumbent President. Later, he came even closer in discussing U.S.-Cuban relations. In a speech aimed at preparing the way for his Florida visit, Reagan said the Ford administration was "working up a prelude to restoring trade and diplomatic relations with Castro's Cuba.'' This was aimed at winning the votes of displaced Cubans who abound in the Miami area, and it was another breach of the spirit if not the letter of the Eleventh Commandment. By Reagan's standards, working toward re-establishment of diplomatic relations with Castro's Cuba is evil, and he made that clear.

If Reagan were the amateur politician he paints himself, these gaffes could be overlooked. It is painfully clear, however, that no man can devote twelve consecutive years of his life (1964 to date in Reagan's case) to politics and government and remain an amateur. Nor was the Reagan entry into the Presidential race spontaneous; it had been carefully planned since the re-election of Richard Nixon in 1972.

Reagan's bid for the Presidential nomination in 1968 was amateurish and never got off the ground. Reagan found it impossible to position himself much to the right of Nixon, a genuine conservative who had sewed up most of the far-right support. But when Nixon was re-elected in 1972 it seemed that all Reagan had to do was wait since the two-term limitation would force an open primary. Nelson Rockefeller, who had resigned as Governor of New York, presumably was also positioning himself for a run at the Presidency in 1976. Reagan and his people perceived that as a race between a "liberal" and a "conservative" Republican, and they were convinced that the GOP was basically conservative. When Spiro Agnew resigned the vice presidency in disgrace, they must have cheered; that removed the sole threat to Reagan's dominance of the right wing of his party.

As Watergate began to unfold and the stories of the Nixon tapes and the coverup attempts dominated the news, a new threat emerged. If Nixon failed to survive his second term, Gerald Ford, who had succeeded Agnew, would become President. Any aspirant to the nomination would have to challenge an incumbent conservative Republican President. The hope in Reagan's camp was that Nixon would last out his term, even if he was battered beyond recognition in the process.

Reagan, who had opposed Nixon four years earlier and who had fought him over the Family Assistance Plan in order to push his own welfare reform program, suddenly began to support the embattled President. So did Nelson Rockefeller, who also hoped to keep Nixon in office until expiration of his term. Neither man was particularly concerned at this point with the damage that might attach to the Republican Party; Nixon's own extra-party committee, CREEP, and the inner circle of Nixon staff members were taking most of the heat. Republicans were angry at Nixon, not their party. But by 1974 Reagan was beginning to feel new pressures. The voters of California had turned down his tax-limitation plan (Proposition One) which was to have been a springboard to the White House. And Nixon's troubles were mounting as it became clearer day by day that he had been involved in the coverup and the criminal activities of several senior staff members. On February 23, 1974, Reagan told reporters in Reno, Nevada, that President Nixon would not be impeached and warned that "there will be a demagogic effort to make Watergate the only campaign issue."

In his prepared address that day he avoided the subject, hammering away instead on his ages-old theme that "demagogues in politics, the classroom, and the communications media are trying to restrict the magic of the market place." At the time the nation was suffering double-digit inflation and the highest unemployment rate since the Great Depression.

In Chicago on March 31 Reagan shared a platform with Nelson Rockefeller at a Republican conference. On that occasion Reagan told reporters that he believed Nixon was innocent of any impeachable offense and should not resign. "He says he's innocent, and I believe him," Reagan said. Then he attacked his fellow conservative, New York's Senator James Buckley, who had called for Nixon's

resignation for the good of the country. "Buckley is not
speaking for conservatives, because nobody has rushed to
join him," was Reagan's simplistic analysis. Rockefeller
stopped short of expressing faith in Nixon's innocence but
said he should not resign.

In May 1974 Reagan told an audience of high school
seniors in Sacramento that he thought Nixon had
demonstrated his sincerity and "made it plain he wants to
bring out all the pertinent evidence and get this issue
[Watergate and coverup] resolved." Perhaps wistfully,
Reagan added: "I think and hope that by 1976 a great deal of
confidence will have been restored."

Reagan's verbal support continued up until the moment
of Nixon's resignation. As a matter of fact, he has yet to utter
his first word of condemnation of the ex-President or the
Watergate mess, presumably to avoid offending diehard
Nixon fans.

Candidate Reagan has redoubled his attacks on big
government, taxes, welfare, and other social programs. He
has not mentioned that voters turned down his radical
scheme to limit taxes in California, and he does not deal with
the realities of his so-called welfare reform law. He has,
however, embraced variations of both concepts in his $90
billion tax-saving scheme, although he might by now wish
he had not launched that boomerang.

Let me say again that I still feel Reagan is an honest man
who is sincerely convinced that his positions are sound. I
find the qualities of honesty and sincerity admirable, but I
suspect they could be attributed to many if not most of the
radical thinkers of history. It is entirely possible to argue
with eloquence and sincerity from false premises, but the
effectiveness of the argument does not make its premises
true.

I believe it is cruel for Reagan to hold out to voters
promises that he knows cannot be kept. I find his willingness
to suggest that America turn its back on its own socially,
economically, and intellectually deprived citizens in the

name of tax reduction is a vivid demonstration of the dark side of the man's personality.

Three Reagan quotes will suffice to justify this charge of cruelty on broader grounds:

On student demonstrations: "If it is necessary to have a bloodbath, let's have it."

On the poor scuffling for free food: "It's too bad we can't have an epidemic of botulism."

On Vietnam: "We should declare war on North Vietnam. We could pave the whole place over by noon and be home for dinner."

Reagan's public record is replete with examples of his indifference to people less fortunate than himself. Former California Assembly Speaker Bob Moretti says he can never recall a display of compassion on Reagan's part. There is no evidence that Reagan has ever allowed concern for human beings to influence his radical desire to slash government spending, at whatever cost in human suffering.

I am gravely concerned about the possibility that Reagan's simplistic, radical politics might disrupt the whole of our national society. I respect my country for its greatness, the nobility of its democratic traditions, and its singular potential for extending peace, freedom, and justice to all men.

I do not believe that Ronald Reagan, a radical anti-intellectual, a government-hater, who appears deaf and blind to our societal responsibilities toward our fellow men, belongs in the highest, most honorable and powerful position of public leadership the world has to offer. Reagan proposes revolution in handling domestic problems. He appears eager to rush to the brink against any foreign threat, real or imagined. His concept of justice is flawed, and his understanding of the dream which has made America great is clouded by personal prejudice and a startling lack of scholarship in a man with such lofty aspirations.

I am a man of certain years with no political ambitions. Life has been good to me, and I have enjoyed success in the private practice of law since leaving public office nine years ago. I have a dear wife, four splendid children, and ten grandchildren to gladden my days. I did not write this book for political or professional or financial reasons. I wrote it as a private citizen with a long background of public service who is alarmed at the possible proliferation of radical Reaganism in the United States.

Reagan told CBS News that he decided to run for the Presidency because he heard a call to serve and he felt he could make a contribution.

That describes rather precisely my purpose in writing this book. I remain certain that the large majority of Americans outside the radical fringe of Reagan's own party will reject the man and his philosophy if given the facts about his record and his radical political thought.

That is what I have sought to do.

Index

abortion issue, 41-42
Agnew, Spiro, 27, 148, 172
Aid to Families with Dependent
    Children, 129, 131
Alioto, Joseph, 101-2
amateurism, 35-39, 47-50
American Veterans Committee, 163
Angola, 30, 171
anti-intellectualism, 68-86
antiwar demonstrations, 103-4

Battaglia, Phil, 166
Bell, Jeff, 52
Berg, Paul, 122
Biddle, Craig, 158-59
blacks, 13-14, 27, 139-43
Blaine, Dan, 110, 111
Bloomingdale, Alfred, 165
Bolton Associates, Arthur, 121
Borax Company, 23, 152
"bracero" program, 143
Brennan, Walter, 164
Brewster, Kingman, Jr., 72-73

Broderick, Helen, 137
Brown, Edmund G., Jr., 146
Brown, Willie, 140
Buckley, James, 173-74
busing, 96, 138

Cagney, Jimmy, 138
California Air Resources Board,
    158-60
California Commission on the
    Status of Women, 147
California Community Colleges,
    77
California State Employees
    Association, 64
California Teachers Association,
    64
Callaway, Bo, 49-50
campus unrest, see student unrest
Cantor, Eddie, 137, 138
Carleson, Robert, 126, 127
Carmichael, Gil, 138
Chandler, Norman, 65

Chandler, Otis, 65
Chavez, Cesar, 143-46
Checkers speech, 161
civil liberties, 97
Clean Air Act of 1970, 158
Commission on Income Maintenance Programs, 134
Committee for the Reelection of the President (CREEP), 173
Community Work Experience Program, 132-33
Conrad, Paul, 65
Cooper, Gary, 138
Cordiner, Ralph, 151
crime, 14, 88-96, 105-6
Cuba, 171-72

Daniels, Caren, 146
Dart, Justin, 165
Davis, Loyal, 165
DeWitt State Hospital, 122
Douglas, Helen Gahagan, 23, 164
Dutton, Frederick, 76
Dymally, Mervin, 139

education, 68-87
Eisenhower, Dwight D., 30
Elk Hills Naval Oil Reserve, 157
energy crisis, 157
Engel, Claire, 153
environment control, 154-60
Environmental Protection Agency, 158
Equal Rights Amendment, 147-49

Family Assistance Plan, 124, 134, 173
Faust, Pamela, 147
Finch, Robert, 72
Ford, Betty, 165
Ford, Gerald, 2, 17, 33, 34, 148, 172
Free Speech Movement (FSM), 70, 71, 98, 100

General Electric Company, 3, 10, 21, 151-52
Gleason, James, 138
Goldwater, Barry, 5, 6, 11, 23, 152-53
Grant, Allan, 72
gubernatorial campaign (1966), 11-15, 20, 38, 98, 99
gun control, 93

Heineman, Ben W., 134
Hitch, Charles J., 78
Holden, William, 164
Hollywood Independent Committee of the Arts, Sciences, and Professions, 163
House Un-American Activities Committee, 163-64
housing, 138-39, 141
Hutchinson, Ned, 146-47

inflation, 14, 55, 57

John Birch Society, 93
Joint Fact-Finding Committee on Un-American Activities, 163
Jordan, Frank, 9, 152
Jorgensen, Earle M., 165

Karloff, Boris, 137-38
Kaye, Peter, 52
Kempton, Murray, 44
Kennedy, John F., 13
Kennedy, Robert F., 83-84
Kerr, Clark, 72
Kuchel, Thomas H., 155

law and order issue, *see* crime
League of Women Voters, 65
Lodge, Henry Cabot, 32
Loeb, William, 162
Los Angeles Times, 65, 75, 102, 119
Lytton, Bart, 164

McBirnie, W. S., 154, 161
McCabe, Charles, 157
McClellan, H. C. "Chad," 44
McGee, Richard, 92
McGill, William J., 81-82
McGovern, George, 170
March, Fredric, 138
Marcuse, Herbert, 81-83
Marx, Groucho, 138
Meade, Gladys, 159
Medi-Cal program, 47-48, 142
Meece, Ed, 127
Mencken, H.L., 51-52, 54
Mendocino State Hospital, 112, 113
Menjou, Adolphe, 164
mental health programs, 108-23
Mexican-Americans, 143-46
Miller, Anita, 147
Miller, James M., 122
mini-memo concept, 24-26
minority problems, 136-49
Moretti, Robert (Bob), 59, 60, 63,
    66-67, 126-28, 133, 175
Moscone, George, 46
Mowbray, Alan, 137
Murphy, George, 9, 143, 153-54

Napa State Hospital, 118, 120-21
National Commission on the
    Causes and Prevention of
    Violence, 98
National Governors Conference
    (1968), 141-42
National Rifle Association, 93
National Sheriffs Association, 90
Nixon, Richard M., 10, 25, 32, 148,
    154, 161, 169, 172-74
Nofziger, Franklyn (Lynn), 49, 165-
    66
nuclear weapons, 30

organized labor, 144-45
Orr, Verne, 85, 167

Palmer, Charles, 29
Panofsky, W. K. H., 80
Parkinson, Gaylord, 12
Pearson, Drew, 27
People's Park battle, 28-29, 101-2
Petris, Nicholas C., 158, 159
Phillip, Irving, 117
Post, A. Alan, 64, 65
poverty, 15, 28, 94, 136-43, 175
presidential campaign (1964), 3, 6,
    9, 11, 23, 152-53
prison sentences, 89, 91-92
Procunier, Roy K., 92
Proposition One, 49, 54, 62-66, 124,
    161, 173
Pueblo incident, 30-31

race riots, 13-14, 27, 140
Rafferty, Max, 74
Raft, George, 138
Reagan, John Edward, 137
Reagan, Maureen, 147, 148
Reagan, Nancy, 150-51, 164-65
Reagan, Neil, 152
Reagan, Ronald
    on abortion, 41-42
    amateurism, 35-39, 47-50
    on Angola, 30, 171
    anti-intellectualism, 68-86
    antipolitics stance, 14, 35-39, 43,
        45
    on antiwar demonstrations, 103-
        4
    autobiography, 19-20, 105, 137,
        160
    blacks and, 27, 139-42
    Borax Company and, 23, 152
    on busing, 96, 138
    conservatism, switch to, 9-10, 21
    on crime, 14, 88-96, 105-6
    on education, 68-86
    on environmental control and
        ecology, 154-60

Reagan, Ronald (*cont.*)
  foreign affairs, 4, 30, 171-72
  as General Electric spokesman,
    3, 10, 21, 151-52
  gubernatorial campaign (1966),
    11-15, 20, 38, 98, 99
  on gun control, 93
  in Hollywood, 22, 150-51, 162-64
  on housing, 138-39, 141
  knowledge of state issues, 39-42
  Medi-Cal program, 47-48, 142
  mental health programs, 108-23
  mini-memo concept, 24-26
  minority problems and, 136-49
  on nuclear weapon use, 30
  on organized labor, 144-45
  peer group, 164-67
  personal life, 22, 23, 150-51, 162-
    64
  personal salesmanship, 15, 16
  poor, attitude towards, 28, 94,
    136-43, 175
  presidential campaign (1964), 3,
    6, 9, 11, 23, 152-53
  presidential candidacy (1976), 2,
    6, 12-13, 33, 38, 49, 161-62,
    170
  presidential nomination, bid for
    (1968), 33, 172
  Proposition One, 49, 54, 62-66,
    124, 161, 173
  on *Pueblo* incident, 30-31
  on race riots, 27, 140
  redwoods issue, 28, 154-55
  reelection (1970), 124
  Roosevelt, F.D., and, 137, 160-61
  Screen Actors Guild and, 137-38,
    162-63, 164
  on segregation and discrimina-
    tion, 136-49
  senatorial candidacy of Douglas
    and (1950), 23, 164
  smog issue, 157-59

Reagan, Ronald (*cont.*)
  "The Speech," 3, 10, 153
  on student unrest, 27-29, 70-71,
    97, 99-105, 175
  on taxes, 47, 48, 51-67, 124, 161-
    62, 170, 173
  television and, 6, 17-19
  on transfer of federal authority to
    states, 52, 135, 162
  on Vietnam War, 103, 153, 175
  on Watergate, 172-74
  welfare reform and, 124-35
  women, discrimination and, 146-
    49
Redwoods National Park, 28, 154-
  55
Reston, James, 4
Rockefeller, Nelson, 172, 173
Romney, George A., 141
Roosevelt, Franklin Delano, 137,
  160-61
Rosenblatt, Irving, Jr., 118
Roth, William, 83
Ruble, A. C. (Cy), 154

Sacramento Bee, 73, 77, 81, 102
Sacramento State College, 77
Salinger, Pierre, 153, 154
Salvatori, Henry, 154
Samora, Julian, 134-35
San Diego State College, 99
San Francisco Chronicle, 78, 79-80,
  121
San Francisco Examiner, 77
San Francisco State College, 99
San José State College, 99
Schlafly, Phyllis, 148
school segregation, 96
Schreiber, Taft, 164
Schroeder, Darrell, 155-56
Schwartz, Milton L., 84-85
Screen Actors Guild, 137-38, 162-
  63, 164

Shaw, George Bernard, 106
Shoemaker, Winfield, 114
Short-Doyle Act, 111
Sierra Club, 155
Slavin, Stewart, 97
Smith, William French, 165
smog issue, 157-59
Sorrell, Herbert, 162-163
Stubblebine, J. M., 118
student unrest, 13, 27-29, 70-71, 97-
    105, 175

taxes, 47, 48, 51-67, 161-62, 164, 170,
    173
television, 16-19
Tennessee Valley Authority, 151-52
Thomason, Mims, 97
Townsend, Ralph, 154
Tuttle, Holmes, 154, 166

unemployment, 14, 125, 129-30
United Farm Workers Union, 143-
    45
United World Federalists, 163

University of California, 78, 79
    at Berkeley, 13, 28, 70-71, 97-98,
        100-2, 104
    at Davis, 80, 81
    at Los Angeles, 99
    at San Diego, 81-82

Vash, Carolyn, 146
Vietnam War, 14, 103, 153, 175

Wallace, George, 15, 33, 95, 142
Wallace, Mike, 161, 165
Warner, Jack, 17
Watergate, 1, 148, 172-74
Wayne, John, 164
Weinberger, Casper W., 86
welfare reform, 124-35
Welfare Reform Act of 1971, 127-29
Where's the Rest of Me? (Reagan),
    19-20, 105, 137, 160
Wilson, William, 165
women, 146-49
Wyman, Jane, 147, 151